THE BLACK MADONNA WITHIN

These four pictures represent steps in the process of Tataya Mato's inner journey:

127. Consciousness turns inward and goes down into the unconscious, the realm of the Black Madonna.

157. The Black Madonna holds the earth in an energy field between Her hands and Her heart.

162. Many people gather in the Earth Cathedral around the Great Mystery, each standing on that patch of inner eternity which not even death can touch.

191. Tataya has found the good and safe place, which her childhood dream promised her.

THE BLACK MADONNA WITHIN

Drawings, Dreams, Reflections

With a Foreword by Marion Woodman

TATAYA MATO

OPEN ❖ COURT

Chicago and LaSalle, Illinois

*Open Court's Dreamcatcher series features personal stories
of discovery, healing, recovery, and inner development.*

✿

OPEN COURT and the above logo are registered in the U.S.
Patent and Trademark Office.

© 1994 by Tataya Mato

First printing 1994
Second printing 1995

Printed and bound in the United States of America.

Library of Congress Cataloging-in-Publication Data
Mato, Tataya, 1939–
   The Black Madonna within : drawings, dreams, reflections / Tataya
Mato : with a foreword by Marion Woodman.
     p.   cm.
   Includes bibliographical references and index.
   ISBN 0-8126-9248-9. — ISBN 0-8126-9249-7 (pbk.)
   1. Mato, Tataya, 1939–   . 2. Religious biography—United States.
3. Black Virgins—Miscellanea.   I. Title.
BL73.M38A3   1994
291.4'092—dc20
 [B]   94-5690
                                       CIP

To All My Relations

It is important to have a secret, a premonition of things unknown. It fills life with something impersonal, a NUMINOSUM. *A man who has never experienced that has missed something important. He must sense that he lives in a world which in some respect is mysterious; that things happen and can be experienced which remain inexplicable; that not everything which happens can be anticipated. The unexpected and the incredible belong in this world. Only then is life whole. For me the world has from the beginning been infinite and ungraspable.*

—C. G. JUNG
Memories, Dreams, Reflections

A Siberian shaman was asked by a traveler if, after the initiation, one could learn still more and received the answer that one could go as far as one liked if ready to pay the price in suffering each time.

—MARIE-LOUISE VON FRANZ
The Feminine in Fairy Tales

CONTENTS

FOREWORD

One jubilant dawn, I was writing at our island home in Georgian Bay. I was trying to describe the inherent radiance of pine trees, green amidst humming rock and diamond-studded water. Love pulsed in nature, pulsed in me, pulsed in every atom of every living thing. I was *in* love.

The phone rang. I was called back to Toronto. Six hours later, I stepped out of a Gray Coach bus into polluted city heat. A monstrous metal hand was ripping up concrete, its fingers gouging out the earth beneath. My body cried out and nearly fell down. I was not only looking at rape; I was experiencing it. Stumbling along on the hard cement, I grieved for the radiance incarcerated beneath.

I arrived at my office and in a stunned state, began opening mail. In the pile was a box of photographs of paintings. The first one my fingers found is figure 120, reproduced here on p. 76—the Goddess imprisoned beneath the concrete city. Tears ran down my face. I knew the painter was painting the radiance that I was attempting to articulate, the same radiance that appears in the dreams of many contemporary men and women.

That was six years ago. Since that time, I have been honored to watch the soul process of Tataya, not as her analyst, but as a woman sharing the search for the conscious feminine. From the beginning, I was impressed by her commitment to her drawing, her wholehearted faith in her inner guides through whatever terrors they might lead. Faced with her personal demons glaring at her from her own pages, she steadfastly painted, day after day becoming increasingly aware of the scars of her childhood abuse.

Into the darkest depths of her physical illness and emotional anguish, light shone. The compassion of the loving Mother manifested in images of intimate cherishing. The abandoned little girl who had not been loved by her personal mother now sat on her Mother's lap, played with her jewels, delighted in her comb caressing her hair. She learned to know herself as a beloved daughter of this Great Mother.

While her process has spiralled through deeper levels of darkness and brighter levels of light, Tataya has been faithful to the gift that is being given to her—a gift that far transcends her personal vision—she continues to draw and paint images that many readers will recognize from their own dreams. In other words, she is creating from the archetypal level, the level at which healing takes place.

In his book *Quantum Healing*,[1] Deepak Chopra, M.D., repeatedly emphasizes that in illness "the real war is not between the head and the heart. Something deeper, in the realm of silence, creates our view of reality." (p. 158). This "realm of silence" is comparable to what Jung calls the archetypal realm. For both Chopra and Jung, the personal ego's relationship to that realm is crucial in healing. As Chopra puts it,

> Thought is linked to thought without end. Our normal experience keeps within this range of ongoing events, which may be infinite on the horizontal axis yet quite shallow on the vertical. It is possible to spend a lifetime listening to the inventory of the mind without ever dipping into its source. Yet, touching the source is how the mind creates its patterns of intelligence. These patterns are at first only blueprints, but whatever they inscribe will hold—they will form our ideas and beliefs about reality. (p. 159)

Rarely do we have the opportunity to observe a healing process as intimately as we can observe Tataya's. In her paintings we can see the original distorted blueprint—the terrified ego encased in its own small perception, paralyzed both by the fear of getting out and remaining locked in. It has no center outside itself and therefore no grounding in a larger cosmos. It has no memory of feeling safe on the lap of the Mother, no memory of feeling whole in her love. We can see Tataya tenaciously persevering in the direction of her fear until out of the "realm of silence" something quite new emerges—the image of the loving Mother. She is the very link who can make the original blueprint whole because if Tataya can surrender to the loving Mother then the wizened ego can be released from its egocentric prison.

This process of growing trust is eloquently portrayed in these pictures. We can see Tataya's perception of reality changing. She moves from the tangled web of her own obsessive fear and symptoms into the flow of her own femininity. At the same time she perceives the anguish of the cosmic feminine still yearning for recognition. It is the ongoing dialogue between personal and impersonal that not only changes the original blueprint but keeps it changing, simultaneously giving new meaning to the personal life.

The dark Madonna present at the center of Tataya's healing process is increasingly appearing in contemporary dreams. Why is she a Madonna? Why is she dark? Why is she appearing in contemporary dreams? Very briefly, let me put forward a few possibilities.

Why is she a Madonna? As an image of femininity, the magnificent woman in these pictures is larger than life. She is more than a beautiful mother. She embodies a divine calm, a concentrated awareness of herself. She is an incarnation of divine energy. Like the Madonna icons of earlier centuries, she has within her the power to bring forth the eternal embodied in the human. Communion with her is communion with the transcendent feminine in ourselves. Like all images born of the concentrating soul—whether they manifest in painting, music, dance, words, or scientific formulas—she is a bridge to the creative source.

Why is she dark? As an icon, the Black Madonna has always carried unique significance. Today, those countries blessed with a Black Madonna find that she has profound powers of healing. And individuals blessed with her presence in their dreams love her at a personal, heart level. The radiance that shines through her darkness is magnetic. Through her austere and loving discipline, she can teach us how to transform dark, opaque, inert matter into the flowing energy of the sacred temple in which we dwell. And honoring our individual temple, we at the same time learn to honor the sacred temple called Earth. Psychologically, darkness suggests that which is still unknown to consciousness. Surely, we need her light to envision our individual selves as living cells at home in one ecological body. Our survival, both as individuals and as a planet, depends on recognizing the light that shines in her darkness.

Why is she appearing in contemporary dreams? In past centuries, she was known to many saints and artists. In the nineteenth century, the Romantic poets perceived her and the French Impressionists wrestled with catching her light in paint. In our century, Einstein saw that inertia was energy and his $E = mc^2$ was the quantum leap that forever changed our relationship to matter. Now she demands, often through illness, that we recognize her. She no longer allows us to think of our own body as an opaque mass nor does she allow us to rape her body with impunity. Dreamers who are being instructed by the Black Madonna are being told in no uncertain terms that there is no time to waste. She startles them out of their narcissism and opens a vision of planetary harmony. Loving her is experiencing light in darkness.

Tataya is not this artist's real name. Tataya is the name given her by the Black Madonna. It means ''rainbow bear.'' Symbolically the rainbow is the connection between Heaven and Earth, between spirit and matter. Tataya's devotion to her own ''realm of silence'' connects her to the images that are the bridge between the timeless and time—the bridge on which healing can happen. Connecting with her imagery, we may discover new light in our own dark corners. We may remember that each of us has an inner bridge to wholeness.

As we move from image to image with Tataya's loving guidance, we can absorb the slow, yeast-like rising of their healing power. The process that worked its sacramental way to health in Tataya may, if we allow it, follow a similar path in us. The darkness of the Madonna may become our light, her stillness, our dancing.

MARION WOODMAN

But though my wing is closely bound
My heart's at liberty.
My prison walls cannot control
The flight, the freedom of my soul.

—JEANNE GUYON (1648–1717)

The psyche is the greatest of all cosmic wonders.   —C. G. JUNG

This book tells the story of my soul. It contains dreams, essays, and active imaginations spanning the years from 1942 to 1993.

At the age of three and a half years, when I was immersed in suffering and embroiled in the senseless, I dreamt for the first time of the realm of THE BLACK MADONNA WITHIN. She received the rejected little girl into an inner place of safety and meaning.

Looking back over my life, fifty years later now, I can see that it has been one long search for THE MOTHER, that is for an abiding and dependable relationship with the Infinite in the midst of the trials of life. Although I did not know it for a very long time, all my inner work had but one goal, namely to find Her again as an adult and to consciously bond and live with Her.

Stubbornly going inward, led by the endless crying of my inner child, I found Her as the Pure Heart of Light shining in the darkness. And when She took me in, I learned that HER BANNER OVER US IS LOVE.

This book is a giveaway to all my relations.

April 22, 1993

CHAPTER 1

Dreams Become Meaningful in Unexpected Ways

Drink the water of thy own well.

—PROVERBS 5:15

When I first met a Lakota Sioux medicine man through a mutual friend in 1988, I remembered the Indian name, *Ta Daya Wado,* that had been given to me four years earlier in a dream (Dream No. 38). I decided to ask him if these words made any sense to him and if maybe they had a meaning.

"Yes," he said after some thinking, "it is old Dakota language and means 'Bearwind' or 'Breath of the Bear,' and the breath of the bear is of course the 'rainbow.' But nowadays in Lakota we say 'Tataya Mato.'" I quickly asked him to write it down for me because I did not believe my ears and wanted to make sure that I had understood correctly. I also wanted to have a record of this. It was a piece of the great puzzle that I have been trying to solve for sixteen years. And the piece fit.

I lost my faith at the age of thirty-two and became an agnostic. To work with the unconscious and to discover the autonomy and religious function of the psyche has been an adventure, a healing experience, and a lovely surprise totally unexpected for me. It is the great find of my life.

Eighteen years ago I discovered C. G. Jung's *Man and His Symbols* in the public library. I read there for the first time about the unconscious psyche and the existence of two subjects within the same individual.[1] It did not make any sense to me at all. But the pictures in the book, the information about dreams, and the description of the individuation process intrigued me to such an extent that I decided to experiment with it. I trained myself to remember my dreams and to write them down. After two years of this, I had three numinous dreams and felt that they meant something for my life (Dreams Nos. 1, 2, and 3). The desire to find out what that could be led me into Jungian analysis. Analysis has been for me truly a "longissima via,"[2] and only more recently have the dreams begun to make sense to me and the pieces of the puzzle begun to fall into place.

My analysis was one long quest for meaning. In the early stages, the dreams were frightening. I dreamt of a big tree in the woods. The tree grew out of a pool of dark water and was cut off from its roots. There was literally a gap between the roots in the water and the rest of the tree. I had nightmares about my parents tormenting and violating me. In my dreams, children were being bitten and murdered. Black children were frozen into submission and total obedience in a freezer box on my maternal great grandparents' farm. There were surprisingly few dreams about World War II and the atrocities during the Russian invasion, which I had seen and experienced in 1945 as a six-year-old in Pomerania, in what was later to become part of Poland. The dreams were so scary that I sometimes called my analyst long distance, just to be in touch with another human being who must have gone through a similar ordeal and knew about the power of the unconscious.

When I began my experiment, I had not expected that the unconscious would mirror back to me the old forgotten or barely remembered childhood traumas. I was then forced to deal with them and to somehow come to terms with a rigid and cruel upbringing in the tradition of strict Northern German Catholicism. The books by the psychologist Alice Miller have helped me in this endeavor. But even before I had become acquainted with depth psychology I had already been comforted by the films of Ingmar Bergmann, especially *The Seventh Seal,* because they articulated suffering. His films have been indispensable mirrors of the human condition for me since adolescence.

For many years it was all darkness and despair and I became afraid of the unconscious forces within. It seemed that I had stumbled, simply out of curiosity, into something that was more than I had bargained for. There were times when I fervently wished I had left well enough alone and not meddled with the energies in my own depths.

But once in a while a dream would come to me that was magical. It would comfort and encourage me through its sheer beauty and I would hold on to it for dear life. Driven by the "only unbearable torture, the torture of not understanding,"[3] I would continue to work on my dreams. I felt as if the mysterious dreams just wanted to be with me. So I simply contemplated them and loved them and lived with them. I could never forget them and felt that they somehow transcended my personal life with its troubles and painful memories, its never-ending stream of duties and my everpresent despair.

One of my analysts told me that these dreams were sent by God. I have always refused to accept that because it had no meaning for me. The silence and the death of God have been very real and bitter experiences since earliest childhood. Intellectual honesty is a necessity for me. I always considered my inner work a solitary experiment, the outcome of which was unknown to me.

Today I know why those great mysterious dreams comforted and helped me. C. G. Jung expresses it well: "the fact is that the approach to the numinous is the real therapy and inasmuch as you attain to the numinous experiences you are released from the curse of pathology. Even the very disease takes on a numinous character."[4]

For years, I felt that I did not understand enough. But I knew that Jung had said: "Often the hands know how to solve a riddle with which the intellect has wrestled in vain."[5] And so I began to paint pictures from the unconscious. They were condensations of my feelings, my emotions. And it gave me great satisfaction to make them.

I used to be an elementary school teacher more than twenty-five years ago in West Germany. In teacher's college I was taught that one does not have to be a professionally trained artist to make valuable pictures because there are many primitive and naive painters in the world who are acknowledged as true intuitive artists. I decided to follow their example and give form to my inspirations. And so I began to make pictures of the dreams and active imaginations. The simple techniques and concepts that I once was taught for doing artwork with children I now use for myself.

My dreams are full of colors. When I began to make the pictures I used tempera paints and acrylics. Later I taught myself how to draw with charcoal. Charcoal is inexpensive and the work goes so much faster than with paint. I like it also because I can rub and smudge it with my fingers and hands which makes me feel as though I'm working with soot. Often I see myself as almost an alchemist. All I have is a sheet of blank paper and a small piece of charcoal. After a few hours of work the black dust has arranged itself into an image that stirs the emotions. Sometimes I even feel as if I were again in my grandmother's kitchen in the old country, where she used to cook in sooty pots and pans over the fire burning in her homebuilt brick hearth. My hands and arms get black from the charcoal, sometimes my face too, and I look a little like a chimney sweep. I have worked thirty hours in one stretch on some pictures. No matter how many times things change on the paper, at some point the mysterious moment arrives when the image that wants to be born is simply there and I cannot touch it again. It seems to me that the pictures have a life of their own and I have to honor that.

The dreams often take me back into the emotions and colors of my childhood. I see things very big in them as if I were a little girl standing before the awe-inspiring beauty of a cherry tree in bloom, or contemplating again the large earth-blackened hands of my grandmother planting seeds in her garden. When I wake up, I am filled with pure joy because what I have seen in the dream was transcendently beautiful.

I have found a way for myself to experience a similar feeling during waking consciousness. When we are small children, our surroundings have such an impact on us that we remember them for the rest of our lives. But who has not experienced disappointment sometimes decades later, when what we remember as large and impressive from our childhood days turns out to be just ordinary and so much smaller? That is because the size of our body in proportion to the world around us has changed.

When I feel a longing to experience intense beauty, I take my opera glasses and walk with them through my house. The opera glasses magnify everything I choose to look at just a few times, just enough that it feels about the size in which a two- or three-year-old child sees it. What I focus on then becomes numinous in the silence of my contemplation: the burning flame of a beeswax candle, overripe speckled bananas in the fruit basket, rock crystals, a slice of homemade bread, the face of my clock, white roses opening up in a vase, pears turning golden on a shelf, hands holding a book. . . . These simple things become awesome through magnification. The other sense impressions too become intensified through concentration: the fragrance of beeswax and smoking flame, the banana smell, the perfume of roses, the ticking of a clock, the wind blowing through the tree by my window, the rustling of a page when it is turned.

I often take my opera glasses along on nature walks and sometimes look at my pictures through them.

Much in the same way I like to listen to Mozart and Beethoven with my Walkman when I paint because it amplifies the sound. I can turn up the volume so that it feels as if I am inside of the music and it surrounds me completely. The supernal beauty which is incarnated in the *Late String Quartets* of Beethoven or Mozart's *Magic Flute,* for instance, then washes over me, consoles me, heals my soul. It is just like in the dreams.

I have a great longing for the transcendental, perhaps because I have seen so much suffering and darkness in my life. And those great mysterious dreams have been for me a way into transcendence. Jung considered a long series of dreams "the context which the dreamer himself supplies,"[6] and in which the dreams make sense. Looking at my own dreams this seems to me to be really so.

Let me give an example. In one of the very first dreams after I had begun analysis, the ocean gave me three slender rings cut out of crystals. They were black on the outside and clear inside. I wore them together with my wedding band on my left ring finger (Dream No. 4). As would happen often in the future my analyst did not know what to make of the dream and neither did I. But fourteen years later another dream came and gave the explanation. In that dream I wore a gold ring on my right hand and the three black rings from the earlier dream had changed to gold. I accepted my fate and acknowledged my vocation as a shaman of the Black Madonna. From now on I would wear the three slim gold bands together with my wedding ring forever (Dream No. 43).

Similarly, the meaning of many formerly incomprehensible dreams has become clear to me within the past year. There is one dream for instance that has always intrigued me. In a mysterious way it seemed to speak of a calling and an important obligation. I have wondered many times where that came from, what it was trying to tell me, and if it was to be taken literally or symbolically. If it was speaking in metaphors to me, what was it really saying? It is dream No. 27, titled "The Sacred Cave of the Brotherhood."

Seven years later the riddle solved itself one day while I was in the process of doing active imagination in the form of a personal ceremony.

I had put my handwoven square Navajo blanket on the ground to set up my earth altar. Each object on this little altar had appeared in a dream. I planned to do a pipe ceremony alone. My new found Native American friends had recently taught me how to smoke the sacred pipe, and I had carved the bowl of my personal pipe into the hands of the Black Madonna the Creator (Dream No. 31). I had also fastened a feather and seven pieces of golden amber with a thong to the pipe, to remind myself of the sacred birds in my dreams (Dreams Nos. 13 and 18) and the dream of the Conjunctio (Dream No. 36). I took this pipe out of its handsewn pipe bag and put it into the center of my altar. Around it I set my dream journal, my bowed psaltery, several choice rocks and crystals, the abalone shell for burning sage and cedar, a braid of sweetgrass, a beeswax candle, my dream rattle, and finally my drum.

I had just begun to smudge myself with the sage and was contemplating my little altar through the smoke, when it suddenly hit me: Aha! *That* is what I dreamed about seven years ago, when my inner journey brought me to the "Sacred Cave of the Brotherhood." Sure enough, there is the square Indian blanket on the ground. And there is the feathered rock: it is of course the pipe, my sacred pipe carved from red pipestone and decorated with a feather. Who would have thought that! I dreamt of a power, the power of life, sleeping in the rock, and *that* can only be the fire. It will wake up when I light the pipe. Its smoke will visibly show the breath, which all beings on the planet share, and the fire in the bowl of the pipe will be a wonderful illustration of the life force. Aha, now we are getting somewhere! This makes sense! We are sharing more with each other than we know! *That* is the *brotherhood!* In my pipe ceremony I will celebrate that all life is One and that like every other being on earth, I am part of a living whole. I will contemplate how deeply I am connected to all my relations: to the people of all colors, races, creeds, and nationalities, to the animals, the plants and trees, the rocks and mountains, the rivers and the oceans, to the air, to all that suffers, to all that lives. In that dream I knew that I would have to paint a picture of the Black Madonna and add it to the treasures on the blanket. Well, it is seven years later and in the meantime I have created many images of Her. Now of course I must frame one for my altar.

For seven solid years I had remembered that dream about the brotherhood and wondered what it meant. I had even made pictures of it. But it simply had never dawned on me that it could have something to do with my destiny, with the obligations arising out of a spiritual inheritance, and with the underlying and secret connectedness of all life forms. My analyst could not help me towards any understanding either. And so the dream had felt to me like a UFO, an unidentified flying object which I had seen for a moment and remembered because I did not know what it was, where it came from, and why it had impressed me so.

But now this piece of the great unsolved puzzle of my dreams had fallen into place all by itself and I was a witness to it.

I once read somewhere that shamans speak to the fundamental helplessness of humanity, and that they first have to test the process of inner healing in the arena of their own existence. They cannot take others where they have never gone. I had to live through innumerable experiences of utter helplessness, shame, and despair, when destiny handed me over to early abandonment, abuses of all sorts, endless years of poverty, humiliation and hunger, illnesses, near death experiences, and the torments of being treated as an untouchable by my peers. Whenever I encounter suffering in others, I think back to those times, and I know how it feels. I can hardly bear to contemplate the fate of my brothers and sisters caught in physical, intellectual, and emotional concentration camps and torture chambers, the crimes against humanity committed all over the world in the course of history and those committed against the planet nowadays, the countless wars, the famines, the dangers of the population explosion, the atom bomb, and our planet's environmental cataclysm. The list is endless and so is the suffering that it stands for. Sometimes in the stillness of the night I hear the children and the animals weep. And I weep with them.

My analysis was basically a solitary quest for meaning. But only in the last year when I learned how to incubate dreams, did I feel that I was getting somewhere. Instead of being passive in relationship to dreams which I often do not understand, I now have a way of actively approaching the transpersonal psyche. I can ask questions and am given answers. I can even reason with the unconscious and talk back as C. G. Jung did in his *Answer to Job* and as he recommends in active imagination. It seems to me now that the experiment which I began eighteen years ago to find out if there really are "two subjects within the same individual" has had a positive outcome. I believe this is what C. G. Jung talks about when he speaks of "the highest and most decisive experience of all, which is to be alone with his own Self, or whatever else one chooses to call the objectivity of the psyche. The patient must be alone if he is to find out what it is that supports him when he can no longer support himself. Only this experience can give him an indestructible foundation."[7]

I would like to share another piece of the puzzle and the moment when it fell into place for me.

It was a mysterious and strangely beautiful thing that happened recently. I had incubated a dream about the meaning of my life and dreamt that I held a lovely, strong child in my arms, which was simultaneously a huge, many faceted, double terminated, clear and pure rock crystal. It had been found fully formed in pipestone red clay and I had to take care of it and bring it up.

Upon awakening I had written the dream down. Then I had gotten up and eaten breakfast with my husband. Since I had a session scheduled that morning with my analyst, we had to make a two hour round trip.

I longed to talk with my analyst about the many dreams which I had incubated in the course of the last month. My husband planned to spend two hours in a park by a river, taking a leisurely walk and watching his beloved birds with binoculars.

The discovery that I could incubate dreams, that is, that I could ask the unconscious all kinds of important questions to which answers would come in the form of dreams, had been very moving and I needed to talk it over with my analyst. I had brought with me my dream journal, the new charcoal paintings, my Plains Indian drum, and my pipe bag. In the four weeks between the last analysis session and this one, I had asked the unconscious for a dream to help me, a dream to comfort me, a dream to show me the next step in my life, a dream to clarify the role of ceremonies for me, a dream to show me how to go about the writings for this book. I had also asked for a dream of strength, a dream to show me what life asks of me, another one about my life's task, and finally for a dream of Blessing.

The dream of this past night had spoken to me about the meaning of my life in the same symbols that the dream of Blessing had done twelve days earlier. That the unconscious had chosen the symbols of clear rock crystals and red clay twice in two weeks, struck me with awe. I had just told my analyst how the new found skill of dream incubation had led me to experience the reality of the transpersonal psyche knowingly and in a dependable way when I reached for my dream journal. But it was nowhere to be found.

I searched everywhere for it and finally remembered that I had put it down for a moment on the roof of our car when I had gotten out of it and realized that I must have left it there. Either it was still on the roof or had fallen off when my husband drove away. My analyst, who was familiar with the location of the park, offered to drive us there in his jeep. We would take the same route that my husband had taken in case the journal was lying somewhere in the street.

We had driven only a few blocks when we spotted it. My analyst stopped the jeep. I jumped out and ran to pick up my dream book. There it lay untouched in the blacktopped street! It had opened to the page on which I had sketched the Black Madonna Chapel in my heart. It was clean and whole. Quite a few cars must have driven on that street during the half hour or so that the book lay there, but not one had gone over it. I felt I was picking up a priceless jewel.

What had just happened to me was that when a synchronistic event connected dreams and outer reality, I had became conscious of it. I instantly remembered and told my analyst one of the three dreams that had led me into analysis sixteen years ago (Dreams Nos. 1, 2, and 3).

At that time I had dreamt of golden green crystals embedded in a blacktopped street. The crystals had been split and broken by the traffic running over them. They wept. But I could not pick them up and save them, no matter how hard I tried (Dream No. 1).

But this morning in my dream that day I had held a huge crystal in my arms. It was an *earthkeeper,* pure, clear, whole, multifaceted, and double terminated. Twelve days earlier, in the dream of Blessing I had already dreamt of many such crystals, except that they had been much smaller, the size of my fingers, arms, and hands. They had grown to full maturity inside of the earth and now lay waiting to be harvested in a ripe golden wheat field on ochre red soil. I was gathering them up by the armful.

The feelings of awe and delight that had accompanied those dreams swept through me again as I picked up my beloved dream journal from the street. It was my treasure, which the traffic had not touched. And on top of that, the dream book as it fell had opened up to the Black Madonna space in my heart like a rose opens its petals in innocence to the light.

I held in my hands the ultimate find of my life: all those numinous dreams in which the transpersonal psyche had responded to my questions. These dreams had given me for the first time in my life a feeling for the "indestructible foundation" within.

I finally had a taste of wholeness. For the moment that unspeakable longing for meaning, justice, and truth which has tormented me since I was a child of three and a half was stilled.

Sixteen years ago, the treasure wept to be seen and redeemed. Today I hugged my dream journal and went back with my analyst to finish our work.

Autumn 1989

CHAPTER 2

My Childhood Dream

. . . the main interest of my work is not concerned with the treatment of neuroses but rather with the approach to the numinous. But the fact is that the approach to the numinous is the real therapy and inasmuch as you attain to the numinous experiences you are released from the curse of pathology. Even the very disease takes on a numinous character.

—C. G. JUNG[1]

The evening twilight has always been the loveliest time of day for me. As a little girl I used to kneel on a small worn footstool by the window in my grandmother's kitchen and welcome the night. As the sun went down, the plum trees and the tall pickets of the garden fence blackened against the red clouds in the West. When I turned around, I saw the dimly lit kitchen transfigured into a place of unearthly beauty, like a mysterious tapestry woven of light and dark. Contemplating this sweet spectacle, I picked up my little bench and walked right into the mystery. From the darkest corner of the room I watched the last light of day fade. The window became very pale and evening turned into night. Then my grandmother would open a door of her hearth in which she kept the fire going day and night. I had been waiting for this moment and moved my footstool into the light that streamed through the open hearth door into the kitchen. There I sat until my bath was ready.

Sitting before the fire the little girl experienced it as a living being. The fire ate the wood, at first charring it, then transforming it into glowing red embers while dancing on it, over it, under it, in it, through it, and all around it in many colors and raining fiery sparks into the ash box below. It made the water kettle hum and whispered in a comforting crackle to the lonesome child looking up to it.

The fire was good to her. It gave her the warmth and mother love she so desperately craved. That fire was the life-giving luminous heart of the night. She felt it reach out to her with blessing hands, embracing her gently, caressing her face, consoling her in her abysmal misery. It helped her live. She was awed by the intensity of its presence and utterly in love with it.

The child was as close to the fire as only shamans can be. She felt that the fire sustained her. And in a mysterious way it also was claiming her. But she had no elders who could have confirmed her intuitions by telling her, for instance, that her ancestors in far away Siberia venerated the fire as a mother and female Divinity. "Mother Fire was imagined as a woman who continually gave birth to girls in the form of tongues of flame."[2] And there was no one around who could have told her about the "Old God" of the Mexican Huichol Indians, Tatewarí, who is the protector of humankind. Observing her devotion to the fire a compassionate elder might have instructed her in the following way:

> Why do we adore the one who is not of this world, whom we call Tatewarí, the one who is the Fire? We have him because we believe in him in this form . . . fire, only fire, flames . . . that is . . . the one who warms us, who burns the brush, who cooks our food . . . Without him, where would we get warmth? How would we cook? All would be cold . . .
>   Imagine. One is in the Sierra, there where we Huichols live. One walks, one follows one's paths. Then it becomes dark. One is alone there walking, one sees nothing. What is it there in the dark? One hears something? It is not to be seen. All is cold. Then one makes camp there. One gathers a little wood, food for Tatewarí. One strikes a light. One brings out Tatewarí. Ah, what a fine thing! What warmth! What light! The darkness disappears. It is safe. Tatewarí is there to protect one. Far away, another walks. He sees it. There he is, walking all alone in the darkness, afraid perhaps. Then he sees it from far away, that light, that friendly light. A friendly thing in the dark. He says, "I am not alone. There is another Huichol. There is someone. Perhaps he has a place for me there, a little warmth." So he speaks. Tatewarí is there in the dark, making it light, making one warm, guarding one. Is it possible to live without such a thing, without Tatewarí? No, it is not possible.[3]

How I wish the child had heard such a story at least once, because the culture into which she had been born did not acknowledge her numinous experience as valid and had no words for it.

Still Tataya lived with the fire and it became the enlightening witness to her life. It saved her soul.

This merits an explanation.

The child grew up in an extremely abusive family and had much physical, emotional, and mental suffering inflicted on her. Every battered child desperately needs to find an adult who has the eyes to see and stands up for the child. Alice Miller calls such a person an "enlightened witness."[4] But until she was an adult not a single human being ever looked at Tataya with the heart, or asked her what she was going through, or defended her. There was no love where she lived.

Since she had no way to escape her agony, the child bonded with the fire, and the fire took pity on her and helped her. During her solitary meditations before the hearth it entered her soul so profoundly that it became her inner teacher and showed her how to live her humanity with dignity and grace in spite of her suffering. That is how the fire became Tataya's enlightening witness and saved her.

When the little girl was three and a half years old the fire spoke to her in a dream and showed her her destiny. She did not know that there were people in this world who are called by dreams and visions to belong to the Holy, but she became one of them. The fire lifted her out of the hopeless situation by giving her the vision of a safe place in the midst of trouble and by showing her how to be a lamp unto herself.

Last year I painted that childhood dream of mine which repeated itself night after night. It clearly called the child to become a "Master of Fire"[5] in the timeless shamanic tradition. The dream was her first shamanic journey into the underworld of the unconscious, the realm of the Black Madonna.

But it would take her fifty years to come to terms with this dream and to work out its meaning. She lived in a culture that gave her no guidance. Her environment had been shaped by the Roman Catholic clergy the members of whom Eugen Drewermann calls "shadow-brothers of the shamans"[6] and who eradicated all traces of shamanism in her European homeland during the last two thousand years, so that there were not even words left for the child to express her encounter with the numinosum. To complicate matters, when she verbalized for herself what she had dreamt anyway, there was no alternative but to use the appalling language of her Christian tradition. Translated into that vocabulary, this most consoling and sacred dream became distorted and a thing of terror to her, as the words reversed the meaning of the dream. The Catholic belief system called what the Divine had decreed for her "judgment day," "condemnation," "Devil," and "Hell." It twisted a simple shaman's initiation dream into monstrous nonsense. "To them Nature is sin and Spirit the devil."[7] And so Tataya had no way to understand what had happened to her. Her loneliness and anguish were boundless.

Half a century later, when she had accumulated enough life experience to think for herself, and had outgrown the church by coming into her own, she understood that as a child she had become transcontextual in true shamanic fashion. With the help of the fire and the dream she had broken through the double-bind situation of her childhood, had made a creative leap out of her suffering and risen to a new level of existence.[8] In her own way and carried by the life force she had become a master of fire, a technician of ecstasy,[9] the creator of her own bliss, the chemist of her own joy.[10] She had gone "beyond the ordinary human condition" by withstanding

1

2

3

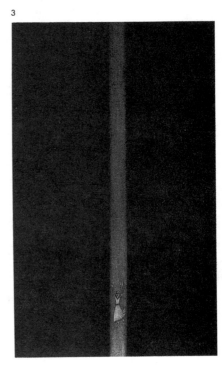

1. In the dream she knows she is dead and ascends into a numinous white light in the sky. There she meets the Divinity face to face. She is shaken by the encounter. The child must give an account of her life and wait to have her destiny decided.

2. The Divine Light decrees that she must descend into the far away realm of fire deep inside of the earth. There she will be given over to a numinous power residing in the depth. She is terror stricken but has no say in what is going to happen to her. She feels herself pushed and falls backwards into a black hole in the ground.

3. She keeps falling and falling through a black tunnel that seems to have no end.

4. Finally she lands safely on her own two feet in a cave filled with fire. She explores the cave, passing by chambers filled with tormented people while she herself walks unharmed through the flames. Afraid of the meeting with the Underground God she clarifies in her mind how to deal with him. She has something to offer to the Force and in return hopes to be treated well.

5. When the Spirit appears, he looks like a column of living fire reaching from the floor of the cave to its ceiling. They speak with each other and work out a mutual agreement. Both sides are satisfied. In exchange for a safe and permanent home and the chance to do meaningful work Tataya will serve the Power forever and keep its house in order.

6. From then on she lives and works happily as mistress of the kitchen in the cave. She tends the fire well and in sooty pots and pans she cooks up food for the God.

4

5

6

the bad winter of being frozen out of all human relationships and become "a participant in the sacred world."[11]

The essay "My Personal Myth" (given in chapter 15 below) contains the dream expressed in the childish language of a tradition far removed from immediate experiences of the numinosum plus a description of my long search for its meaning in the context of Jungian psychology.

As long as I can remember I have been driven by a passion for the ineffable and a fundamental need not just to live, but to understand life and to transcend its horrors. We need to turn somewhere for consolation when misfortune and suffering overwhelm us and there is no respite and no one to help. How else can one live gracefully with loneliness, affliction, and the omnipresence of death? What is one to do when all exits are closed and one does not know what to do anymore?

In hopeless situations I instinctively turn inward, exactly as the child did. She sat before the hearth in solitude and stillness, looking at nothing but the fire, contemplating its mystery and beauty with undivided attention, waiting for its transpersonal dimension to reveal itself to her. She intuitively knew how to incubate a dream.

This passion to live the life of the soul has remained with me, perhaps because I am heartbroken and dependent on the unconscious to help me. I have seen too much and I am too crippled to bear my misery without dreams, rapture, the fire. A life lacking transfiguration would be a dreadful thing to have to go through.

The great presence within has become my friend. I feel carried and unconditionally supported. This core-experience of my existence I like to call the Great Mystery. In my dreams it wears the face of the Black Madonna.

I feel that living with one's dreams is nothing out of the ordinary since people in other cultures do it all the time. The unconscious is indigenous to every human being. And dream incubation is a simple process that can be learned. The Transpersonal Psyche, our deepest Self, constantly reaches out to us as C. G. Jung has shown. The Black Madonna is waiting for us to turn inward so that She can help us.

GREAT MYSTERY BEFORE ME.
GREAT MYSTERY BEHIND ME.
GREAT MYSTERY TO THE LEFT OF ME.
GREAT MYSTERY TO THE RIGHT OF ME.
GREAT MYSTERY BELOW ME.
GREAT MYSTERY ABOVE ME.

GREAT MYSTERY ALL AROUND ME.
GREAT MYSTERY WITHIN ME.
I BELONG TO THE GREAT MYSTERY.

Spring 1993

CHAPTER 3

Terrifying Experiences Lead to a Heightened Awareness of the Transcendental

Lord, how come me here,
Lord, how come me here,
Lord, how come me here?
I wish I never was born,
I wish I never was born![1]

One evening several months ago I switched on the television. There on the screen Kathleen Battle appeared singing softly and plaintively the old American spiritual quoted above. As I listened, I felt such a wrenching pain in my chest and arms that my body doubled over and I could not help but weep. Echoing within my soul and body was the abysmal pain of the tormented woman who once created this heartrending lament. Her sorrows touched mine. She was my sister in extreme affliction. She was me and I was she. What she sang was the truth.

Memories came flooding in. As I recall them now, I can see myself again in the old country, in Pomerania, in 1945.

It is late one evening in early spring. I am standing with my little sister in an open field between my grandmother and my mother. Close by are other women. The sky flames red. Our hometown is burning, having been set ablaze by the Russian soldiers. We are looking at a second fire in front of us. The soldiers have torched a barn. And as the bright flames lick the sky, I see rafters fall and black beams slipping. My heart pounds. We are all weeping. The old women moan. Some hold each other by the hands.

It is midmorning on another day. We are walking in a long trek with many people on a country road. We are very tired and thirsty. Dead German and Russian soldiers are lying everywhere in the ditches. Some have their eyes open and stare at me. Those glassy eyes scare me so. I clench my teeth so that I don't faint and cause trouble.

As I listen to Kathleen Battle, the memories intensify and I feel again shaken by gut-wrenching fear. I hear women and children scream. I am one of them. The Russian soldiers have just murdered the estate owner before our eyes. He was a kind man and had given us refuge. When the soldiers checked the men's hands for calluses and other signs of manual labor, his were clean and soft. And so he had to die.

Now they have lined us all up for execution. We don't know why they make us wait. A half-drunk soldier with a German shepherd at his side is guarding us at gunpoint. I see the neck of a vodka bottle, closed with a cork, sticking out of his right coat pocket.

Suddenly it seems that he cannot take our crying and sobbing any more. Something inside of him snaps. In broken German he yells: "Raus!" We run as fast as we can. My little sister loses one of her shoes. She has to walk now with only one shoe. A few days later we will find out that the soldiers in their madness killed every person who stayed behind on the estate, even the blind woman and the paralyzed one.

We find a wheat stack in an open field and crawl into it. We stay there huddled together, safe for a while from the soldiers who forever hunt for women.

It is noontime and another day. We have barely escaped from Russian soldiers who followed us across the fields still dotted with patches of snow. They shot at us many times and missed, because we were just out of range of their bullets. My grandmother has led us to safety on a narrow path through a wet peat bog. I am still trembling from listening to the anguished screams of the young girl whom the soldiers raped as we climbed over a weather-beaten picket fence and ran away. The sun is burning down on us from a clear sky. I feel ever so hot and thirsty. We are all exhausted and scared. Finally we reach a small house, half-hidden behind bushes and a low wooden fence covered with green creepers. My mother knocks at the door. An old woman opens it. She brings out a pail of fresh well water and a lovely china cup. The white cup has a pale rose-colored rim and is decorated on the inside with tiny scattered roses. We all drink from that cup one after the other. I am already six years old, but at this moment I taste water for the first time consciously: cool, clear, life-giving water!

A few days later we are back in our hometown. It is evening. Russian soldiers poke me with their guns and hit me with their rifle butts. They have come into our little house which is still standing. It has been looted. The windows are broken. The piano has been smashed with an ax. In the cellar each and every glass jar that held canned fruits and vegetables lies shattered on the floor. And now the soldiers are back. After having brutally murdered our bedridden neighbor by driving a nail through the top of her head with a hammer, they interrogate and torture my grandfather.

He sits in the middle of the room on a chair. A light shines on him. His head is bent. Blood flows in streaks over his face and drips slowly from his white curls. The soldiers are standing behind him. Their voices are hard. Their laughter is mean. My stomach is cramping upwards into my chest and my teeth chatter with terror.

At dusk on the following day, I sit with my grandmother, mother, and little sister on the wooden floor in a corner of a strange house. There are other women with us in the room. My mother's best friend, who squats at her side, wears a silver locket in the shape of a small prayer book on a chain around her neck. She opens it and takes out a miniature rosary made of sterling silver. We all pray together. We are terrified of the Russians who roam the streets, loot the houses, rape the women, torture the men, and kill whomever they please. We are praying that they won't find us. But they do.

They break in the door. They brutally interrogate us at gunpoint. Then they order the women to hand over their wedding bands. My mother's is slim and made of yellow gold. But my grandmother's is wide and made of rose-red gold. And she always wears it on her right middle finger.

A white candle flickers and sizzles on the dark wooden table. Shadows dance on the walls. A soldier lifts his left hand towards the light to look at his index finger. It is covered with shimmering wedding rings. I shiver.

After that, one of the Russian soldiers returns to visit us during the day on several occasions. He has fallen in love with my blue-eyed, blond-haired sister who is four years old. He threatens my mother with his plan to take the child away from her and back to Siberia with him if she does not give him a gold watch. She does not have one.

During the night I hear her whisper to my grandmother. They think I am asleep. My mother has decided to drown me and my little sister in the lake and then herself if the soldier does not change his mind.

As Kathleen Battle finishes the spiritual and my hand turns off the television, I allow one more memory to come up.

My little sister and I are climbing in the ruins of our neighborhood, hunting for treasures. We have heard of a villa around the corner, where one can find gold coins that were hidden in the ground by people who wanted to protect them from the Russians. And so we go there.

As we enter the front yard, I immediately become entranced by the lovely scent of a huge jasmine bush in full bloom. Thousands of snow-white blossoms make it transcendently beautiful.

I have never seen anything like it. I dive underneath the branches and get into this almost sacred cloud of fragrant blossoms. I take the flowers into my hands, enjoy their perfume, count their petals, and contemplate their golden centers. I climb through the branches. I become aware of the sweet hum of innumerable bees that are collecting their honey from the bush.

My little sister calls me over to show me what she has found. I hope it is the gold we have been looking for. When I look, I see a corpse instead.

It is a woman who burned to death when the Russians set her house on fire a few days ago. She looks so small. Her clothes have all burned off and the skin is awfully black and brown. Most of her hair and ears are gone. She wears grey hand-knit socks, which are charred at the tops and sunken into the flesh. But the soles look almost normal. A sickening chill overcomes me.

I run back into my white fragrant cloud. I listen to the bees. I delight in the aroma of the blossoms. I climb through the branches. I play with twigs and pebbles in the dirt. My little sister does the same. Then I walk over to the burnt woman and contemplate her again.

I go back and forth.

Inside the jasmine bush I am safe and forget the nightmare on the other side. I blot it out. I abandon myself to the unearthly beauty of the holy, blooming bush. This sacred cloud is a fountain of living strength, a source of blessing. Like my first dream it caresses me and wipes away my misery and despair. It sings to me in the exquisite hum of honey bees. It envelopes me with a soft shawl of shadows and filtered light. It protects me by pulling its snowy veil of blossoms over me and wrapping me into it.

The child's inborn sense of the sublime, like an instinct, has taken over and transported her to a good and safe place beyond life and death.

Is this what happens when the central core of a human being is touched and activated through intolerable suffering?

The leap into inwardness made it possible for the little girl to embrace life, even when she was walking through the valley of the shadow of death. The instinctive vision which connected her to the transpersonal helped her live with dignity and grace in wretched circumstances, as her first childhood dream had done before.

Thinking back to that child, I have often reflected on the following questions which I consider to be of utmost importance:

How do human beings deal with their fundamental helplessness in extreme situations? How do they comfort themselves when they are hopelessly overcome by affliction and there is no one to turn to for help and no consolation any more? How do they transform their agonies when life goes on and they need to keep their dignity and sanity intact? What creative leaps occur in the psyche of a gifted human being who suffers because he or she is cut off from the possibilities of culture, education, and refinement through adversities or lack of funds? What happens to a thinking person who lacks the means to get psychological help after traumatic experiences and is left to his or her own devices on the quest for meaning and wholeness?

For most of my life I have been in these circumstances. Like many of my brothers and sisters all over the world, I was and still am forced to live at the edge.

It would be carrying things too far to go into all the details. Suffice it to say that the trials of my life included abandonment, physical and emotional abuse, molestation, loss of my homeland, refugee camps, illnesses resulting from prolonged semi-starvation during late childhood and adolescence, grinding poverty for many years, beatings from my father and mother until I was twenty-three years old, crude mind control, and endless double binds. The trials continued after my immigration to the U.S., with menial jobs, isolation from cultural and intellectual life, three miscarriages, the loss of loved ones, cancer, and many other sorrows. A deep concern of mine was that I, who had grown up abused, would not pass on the suffering to my husband and son. Part of my inner work consisted of breaking the vicious cycle and transforming it into a cycle of blessings.

The miseries of my life have sharpened my sense of the terrifying seriousness of the human condition and taught me the primacy of inwardness. I have no illusions about what can happen to each and every one of us at any time and to the world as a whole.

And so I feel that a problem which deserves utmost attention is the question of how to nurture and bring to maturity one's inborn sensitivity to the transcendental in order to find the certainty which allows one to live abundantly in spite of everything.

I have always been intensely curious to find out how others have come to terms with the tragedies of life. And since I love to read, once in a while I have come across a book written by a kindred spirit who lived in another time and place, but who was spontaneously sensitive to the numinous. I have held on to these books which provide a meaningful perspective to my existence and have made them a part of my life. I feel deeply connected to the authors in a way that really matters and helps me live.

These books are my lasting companions. In reading them I feel as if I am holding a living part of my spiritual ancestors in my hands and I hear their voices speaking to me as intimately as my own thoughts. In some mysterious way my essence meets theirs and pure joy in which all sorrows drown wells up from within.

It is much like listening to certain pieces of classical music, for time and space do not exist anymore when I abandon myself to the sublime music of Beethoven's *Fidelio,* the Ninth Symphony, or the Late String Quartets. My soul becomes still. I contemplate the ineffable, incarnated in the music, inexpressibly beautiful and alive, and now reverberating upon my own sense of the essential and imperishable.

In the last chapter of his book *Cosmos,* Carl Sagan describes the pleasure of making contact with one's ancestors through reading:

> How ignorant we are of our own past! Inscriptions, papyruses, books time-bind the human species and permit us to hear those few voices and faint cries of our brothers and sisters, our ancestors. And what a joy of recognition when we realize how like us they were![2]

I experienced this joy of recognition, when some time ago I came across a few words written by the philosopher Plotinus, who lived more than seventeen hundred years ago. I was struck by the fact that his experience closely resembled mine. Since then I have often repeated to myself this exquisitely beautiful and comforting sentence, while focusing on the mystery of the psyche which it evokes:

THERE IS ALWAYS A RADIANCE
IN THE SOUL OF MAN, UNTROUBLED
LIKE THE LIGHT IN A LANTERN
IN A WILD TURMOIL OF RAIN AND TEMPEST.

Autumn 1991

CHAPTER 4

First Active Imaginations

Through suffering the ego becomes conscious of the Self.
—MARIE-LOUISE VON FRANZ
C. J. Jung, His Myth in Our Time[1]

The following two series of pictures were painted with tempera on paper in 1974 and 1975. They are my first attempts at active imagination.

At that time I was suffering from nightmares in which I had to fight for my life. In many of them my parents were persecuting, violating, torturing, and trying to murder me. In one dream my mother was called "Sister Rochana." This pun combined the English word *sister* (a Catholic cleric) and the German *Zitterrochen* (devil fish or electric ray) into a name for her.

But I knew that no matter how much my parents had once abused me, I now was an adult and on my own. Life was asking me to take responsibility for what went on in my own unconscious. I had to try to come to terms with that to the best of my abilities. At the time I also was trying to cope with culture shock. I had followed my husband, a working man, to the New World out of love. When he was repeatedly laid off from work, I became trapped in menial jobs, working for minimum wage or less. I had believed in the myth of social equality and a classless society and now found myself looked down upon and treated with disrespect because of our low status. In addition I had the problem that an essential part of me can breathe and flourish only when nurtured by the literature and music of the Old World and I had no access to books and tapes at the time. This suffering expressed itself in an overwhelming homesickness for the Romanesque cathedrals of Europe, of all things. But I never had the means to go back and let my soul take refuge in them.

Only slowly did I learn to accept these sorrows as a normal part of my new life. Years later I found a book which helped me in that process. As I read about the lives of other people like me, I saw my own situation reflected in the book's pages time after time and felt connected to the people about whom I was reading.[2]

In the meantime, my despair felt like a monster, the tentacle roots of which stretched far into my childhood and that had now settled in my gut. I called it the *grey octopus of emptiness and unfullfillment.* When in my initial active imaginations I painted this personal monster of mine as well as the impersonal mother-monster of the dreams, I experienced for the first time the way in which images begin to move and transform themselves when inner work focuses one's attention on them. This was quite an experience as you will see in the pictures that follow.

Around the time that I dreamt of the mother-monster, I also had a dream in which a luminous football-shaped object hovered in the night sky. It consisted of a dark core surrounded by a rainbow in many hues of red. Its outer rim was a halo of golden light. It was huge. It shone in the darkness and filled me with such reverence that all I wanted to do in the dream was to go with it wherever it would go. As this fateful star floated ahead of me, I followed it through the night with utter devotion.

When I painted the vision, I again witnessed the unfolding and transformation of dream images during the process of active imagination.

These first experiments with active imagination were an unforgettable experience. I found that when I dared to face a dream and stay with an image, I was able to see it move and transform itself in my hands and under my eyes. It was as if the unconscious was giving me a lesson in hope, as if my suffering contained a great spiritual opportunity. It was as if the unconscious was saying to me: "Nothing is fixed forever. Life is change. Trust the life force in your own inner depths because to change is to be in harmony with nature." C. G. Jung might have said in this context, "We must be able to let things happen in the psyche."[3]

Spring 1993

7

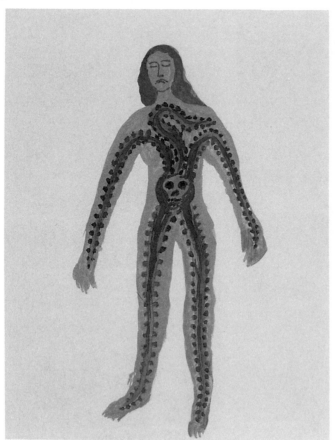

8

9

7. The woman's whole being is filled with monstrous despair. She cannot get away from it, no matter where she turns or what she does. She feels she is at its mercy, immobilized from within, and stagnating.

8. This is *Sister Rochana*, the mother-monster of her dreams that lives in her unconscious. Standing in a safe place on the shore by the ocean, she can take a look at this thing with the help of her analyst.

9. Filled with hope that she can come to terms with this demon, the woman prepares her fishing pole with bait.

10

11

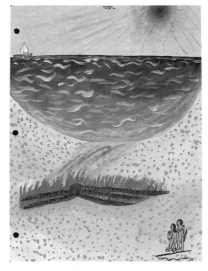

12

10. The unconscious likes the attention given to it. This means that the monster swallows the bait, hook, line, and sinker. Once pulled onto the land, its power weakens, its hold over the woman collapses.

11. With her analyst at her side, the woman keeps her distance from the creature, watching as it burns itself out.

12. When she feels it is safe, the woman walks up to the monster. A mysterious luminous power, which had appeared to her in a dream, stands by her and protects her. With sword in hand, the woman begins to finish the monster off.

13

14

16

15

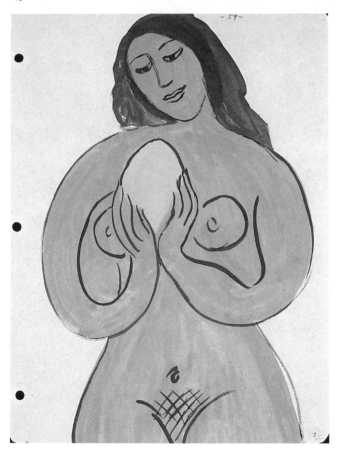

13. She gives it her all because she wants to put an end to the destructive activities of that death-bringing force.

14. As she strikes the death blow, she sees gold gleaming deep down in the awful mess.

15. It is an egg of pure gold. And when she holds it in her hands close to her heart, it grows bigger and bigger in a mysterious way.

16. A little black girl hatches from the egg and greets her with a smile of recognition and affection.

17

18

19

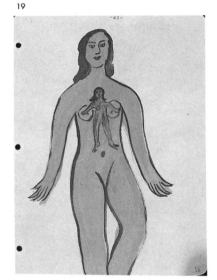

17. The child begins to talk and tells the woman that she is her long lost twin. A long time ago they were born in Africa. As they played together on the beach one day, a monster reached out of the depths, grabbed her, pulled her under, and devoured her. At that moment the woman lost half of her soul. Now the child demands to be reunited with the woman: "You must swallow me."

18. The woman feels that the child tells the truth, and without hesitation eats the little one.

19. And so the long lost twin finds her way into the woman's heart.

20

20. Loved, protected, and cherished by the woman the child grows fast.

21. Soon her twin is the same size as she is and as important to her as she is to herself. Each lives with the other. Each has taken on some of the other's skin color and characteristics and blended them with her own. The two sisters, living one within the other, dance and sing their freedom.

22. Often the woman now dreams that she is bathing and washing her hair. She spends much time contemplating the changes taking place in her own inner depths.

23. In many of the woman's dreams her little son is fighting for his life. These dreams usually take place in a church setting. The woman has to save the child from the priests who try to murder it when they go to mass. The priests have skulls, not live heads with eyes, ears, nose, mouth, and hair like other people. In the pews they have installed traps with switchblades and poisoned needles that shoot out to kill the child when the woman kneels down to pray holding her son in her arms. During active imagination now the woman sees the boy caught in a bleak prison, grey and empty. Suddenly the door flies open, the child is free and runs into his mama's arms to be hugged.

21

22

23

24

25

26

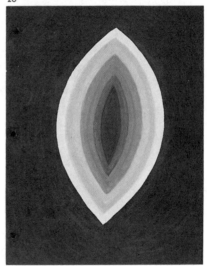

24. The woman now dreams that she is a full-blooded east European gypsy, freedom-loving, earthy, colorful, who takes her power and plays the violin masterfully and with abandon.

25. Thankful for her life she gives homage to the earth.

26. This is the luminous football-shaped object hovering in the night sky that I saw in the dream. It has a dark core surrounded by a rainbow consisting of many different reds and a rim of golden light.

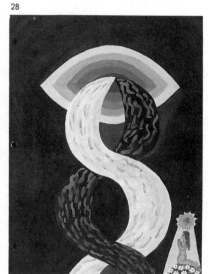

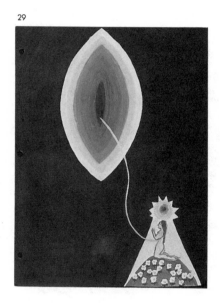

27. Awed by the apparition, the woman contemplates it with devotion.

28. As she focuses her attention on it, it opens up and emits two rivers of life, a bright one and a dark one, which intertwine.

29. A golden cord grows between her and the dark core.

30. The woman sees that all life comes out of the great vulva and returns to it again to be recycled.

31

33
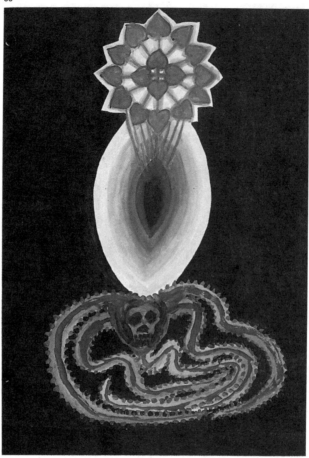

32

31. She witnesses the life cycles of people, animals, trees, and other things. All must journey through birth, growth, maturation, reproduction, old age, and death back to the source from which they came.

32. Suddenly a beautiful lady with skin like golden honey appears out of the darkest part of the vulva. She looks at the woman with kind eyes and sends a stream of light towards her.

33. In a mysterious way, the woman does not know how, the vulva absorbs the mother-monster and transforms its molecules into a sacred plant with heart-shaped leaves.

34

35

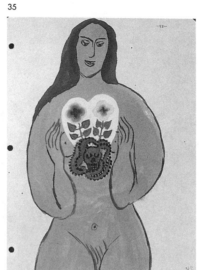

37

36

34. This process of transformation takes place in the woman's interior. The new growth feeds on her old troubles and thus gives them meaning.

35. Now the old mother-monster is the much needed fertilizer for the blossoming. Two lovely flowers unfold. One is blue, the other red. They bloom within a heart-shaped light.

36. The woman feels herself loved and protected by the radiant vulva which now resides in her heart and generates light.

37. Suddenly the vulva changes into a huge living beating heart. The woman watches her own small life arise out of that heart, take its course and return into it.

38

39

38. Now she becomes aware that this heart which glows
in a symphony of red hues, from rosy pinks to bright
oranges and fiery reds to a deep violet, belongs to the
golden-skinned lady and overflows with love and
compassion towards her.

39. She begins to experience her creativity as part of the
creative force in the depth of her own unconscious.

40. Inner work has led the woman to connect with different aspects of her personality in the unconscious. She now experiences an inner family, so to speak.

41. A new dream has come to her. She dreams of being in a sacred place of nature. Between four grassy hills a golden light streams out of the earth. In the center stands a child, a little boy dressed in white. With a sweet clear voice he sings an aria from Handel's Messiah: "He shall feed His flock like a Shepherd; and He shall gather the lambs with His arm, and carry them in His bosom, and gently lead those that are with young" (Isaiah 40:11).

40

41

CHAPTER 5

The Vampire and the Black Madonna

The Vampire and the Black Madonna is a series of twenty-four charcoal drawings done between August 20 and September 2, 1982.

42

42. The unsolved problems of her existence and her desperate need to be in a place where she is safe and cannot get hurt anymore have driven the woman into the solitude of spiritual and intellectual life. Now it turns out that living too much in her head and being too high up spiritually are real afflictions too. It feels to her as if a vampire is holding her in his claws, draining all energy and color from her life.

43

44

43. She is in a precarious position and weeps in helpless despair. as her blood, symbol of the life force, runs out of her, leaving her feeling depleted and depressed.

44. The woman's internal suffering calls forth the instincts from her own inner depths. She now dreams often about animals that have come to be with her and help her.

45

46

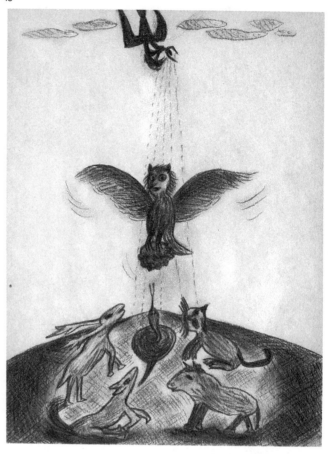

47

45. A deer, a horse, a cat, a buffalo, a snake, and a blue-green owl have come to her in her dreams with messages of deliverance. They are looking for a way to reconnect the woman with the earth, and thus to restore her vitality to her.

46. But before healing can take place, it is necessary that the woman gets in close touch with the earth somehow. But how can she possibly do that up there in the clouds? The animals know that they must do for her what she cannot accomplish herself (Dream No. 9). And they ask the owl to take a clot of pure black earth up to the woman.

47. The owl prepares that ball of dirt, flies up into the rain of blood and tears and brings the woman's feet to the ground.

48

49

48. Contact with the soil renews the woman's strength. She bounces out of the vampire's grip and is free at last. The owl hits the bloodsucker over the head. He loses his power, gets weak and dizzy, and falls down.

49. Being able to rely on her instincts and intuitions, her natural inner tools of self defense, are a saving grace for the woman. The helpful animals of her dreams are metaphors for these inborn powers. They are her wise and dependable friends who go with her everywhere; they are an acknowledged part of her existence now.

50

51

52

50. In the meantime, night has fallen and new dreams have come to the woman. Stars and moon have risen. The animals help her to come to terms with her past by helping her claim for herself the energies that fate had taken away from her but which are her birthright. And so they stomp on the vampire's belly to make him throw up the stolen blood and give it back. Then they stomp some more for punishment.

51. The woman and her friends light a big fire and cook the reclaimed blood and her past life experiences in a cauldron over the flames (Dream No. 12). This process purifies the energies and distills out of her past an essence which is a mysterious, pure joy of life.

52. And so she continues her journey, empowered and protected by the instinctual layers of her psyche. She trusts in the natural flow of the life force (Dream No. 17), and for the first time since she was a child, she feels vibrantly alive.

53

54

55

53. As she goes on with her journey, that is, as she simply goes on with her life and inner work, she meets the blessing hands of the Black Madonna in several dreams (Dream No. 31). These Divine Hands, the life force itself, hold her dear, cherish her, acknowledge her life as valid and precious in all its phases and support her reliably from within.

54. She is surprised to see the sun, the moon, and the stars suddenly line up in a preview of things that are still hidden in the future (Dream No. 36). She once dreamt of a huge hand coming out of the sky, carrying fire and lighting seven sacred lamps filled with oil in a temple. This hand from above is now met by a black hand from below. Both hands accept each other and hold on to each other in a new covenant.

55. While this is happening, the woman witnesses the cosmic dance of sun, moon, and stars. Flashes of lighting from above and below meet before her and connect Heaven and Earth. The woman is a part of it all and submits to the powers in the depth of her own soul which call her to her destiny (Dream No. 8).

56

57

58

59

56. The woman now meets her inner man and they play ball together in the rain. This symbolizes a coming together of outer and inner, of above and below (Dream No. 18).

57. Together with her inner beloved, the animals, and all other beings the woman now happily celebrates life on the big mother body of our planet (Active Imagination No. 29).

58. By living with her inner man, the woman has created an elegant mirror for the Black Madonna, made of understanding and clear thinking, in which She can contemplate Her face. Since the Goddess can not bring forth such a mirror by herself, She treasures this utterly human gift and depends on it.

59. The woman's struggles and much inner work have brought her and her companion to a promised cave hidden away in the mountains (Dream No. 27).

60

61

60. They enter the cave and discover to their great amazement that they have come home and belong to a tradition as well as to the great web of life, which connects all living beings on our planet in one great brotherhood. They add their own gift to the treasures on the blanket: a homemade picture of the Black Madonna (Dream No. 27).

61. They now witness the Mass of the Black Madonna, a process that takes place in the depths of the psyche (Dream No. 21). The integration of earthiness and spirituality appears to them as a shaft of light which fuses bread and wine into one on the altar (Dream No. 28).

62. And now the woman remembers a dream in which the earth split open in the shape of an even-armed cross, revealing a hidden treasure house of pictures (Dream No. 19). Those pictures are the woman's dreams and active imaginations, which she will faithfully record and paint in the years to come.

63. The fact that through constant practice it has gotten easier for the woman to do inner work has been expressed through an image in her dream: whenever she wants to, she can now climb into the depths and bring up a picture. And so she realizes that her creativity and inspirations emanate from the unfathomable depths of the human soul, and not from a source outside or above her as was traditionally thought.

64. The woman and her inner man labor hard to carry the Mirror of the Black Madonna to the White Church (Dream No. 20), that is into that inner space of her personality which has been shaped by her upbringing. Since intense love for this earth and a sincere appreciation of the natural side of life were lacking in her tradition, the work requires much courage (Dream No. 39). But the people, the components of the woman's psyche, are waiting and the dreams, the impulses coming from within, drive her and leave her no choice.

65. In the inner sanctum of the woman's soul, the Mirror of the Suffering Black Goddess is given the place of highest honor (Dreams Nos. 20 and 23). There the Black Madonna is loved unconditionally and venerated by the people: earthiness and the senses have been fully accepted into the woman's existence. As a result of this—and it feels like grace—she has her vitality back, life is fresh and invigorating, and her whole being rejoices in the vivid colors of the world.

CHAPTER 6

The Octopus and the Black Madonna

The *Octopus and the Black Madonna* is a series of ten charcoal drawings done between September 13 and October 1, 1982.

66. See Overleaf

67. She succeeds after much inner work in pulling the bad stuff out of the unconscious and into the daylight. Now she can take a look at it and deal with it. There is new growth taking place deep within as she works her way through the dreams and active imaginations.

66

66. Painful memories, undigested traumas, unwept tears, and inaccessible early life experiences exhaust the woman from within. She feels at the mercy of an affliction that has no face or name, and which announces its presence as depression. *That thing* sits inside of her. It feels deadly and seems to run her life. But the icicles of despair have begun to melt in the cave of her heart.

68

69

70

71

68. The woman has learned to accept the detours and unplanned turns of life and to submit to the often strange and at times frightening ways of nature. This surrender has brought her the insight that what she used to consider meaningless suffering has really been a necessary condition for greater maturity. It has mellowed her, made her more compassionate, and deepened her knowledge of the human condition. As a result she has become aware of her irrevocable bond with all who suffer.

69. She now has the strength to voluntarily accept the process of being cooked in the heat of her emotions. Survival has not been enough. Becoming conscious of and integrating the many traumas, torments, and miseries of her existence results in an increase of energy and inner peace. She learns that getting by and living with zest are two different things.

70. During this slow growth process her dreams mirror back to her the changes that are taking place in her unconscious as a result of steady conscious inner work. She begins to walk on her troubles, so to speak, hugging the bird, her creative spirit, close to her heart.

71. She is rewarded with increasing energy from all sides, from her conscious inner work as well as from the deeper layers of the psyche. Sometimes she now feels consoled and helped from within, supported by a pure and mysterious joy.

72

73

72. But mostly she feels torn apart by the tension created through the demands of her family life and workaday duties, and the needs of her inner world. She has a hard time trying to balance the opposites, and struggles to do justice to both sides without neglecting one or the other. "The bringing together of opposites for the production of a third: the transcendent function" has become a vital necessity for her as she realizes that "At this stage it is no longer the unconscious that takes the lead, but the ego."[1]

73. Many dreams are telling the woman now that the Black Madonna supports and guides her and her loved ones from within. And so they all journey together through life, holding on to each other and singing most gratefully together.

74

75

74. Pausing for a rest on their way, they take each other by the hands and looking at each other, they dance a circle dance together to the beat of their own rhythm, to the music of their own tune, and are reconciled to what life has given them.

75. Having accepted the hand that life has dealt her, the woman plays it well by leading a simple life, close to the soil and her soul's indigenous roots, that is, close to the unconscious and her dreams. And so the Earth, life itself, the Black Madonna, has become her mother. She feels she is the prodigal daughter who has finally come home.

CHAPTER 7

The Suffering Black Madonna

T*he Suffering Black Madonna,* a picture of the Black Madonna holding a crucified woman in her lap, was painted two years after I had dreamt the scene (Dream No. 26). While working on it, I poured all my inner and outer sufferings of that time into the picture. I created a mirror of Her, who is the abandoned outcast and leper woman of my dreams, as well as an image of the tortures that a human being endures as a participant in the drama of Divine Transformation.[1]

The Black Madonna in this picture is the Woman of Sorrows. Wounded by our transgressions, despised, rejected, cut off from the land of the living, she is helpless to change her situation. She weeps in endless silence. But her whole body speaks louder than words through the oozing sores of her agony. Hopelessly alone, she holds on to the crucified woman, looking towards her for help. This situation is almost unimaginable and really too horrible to contemplate. All around the Black Madonna blood-red roses bloom, northern lights are flashing, the blue-green owl of my dreams watches, bones in the soil change to compost, stars appear in the dark sky. And the crucified human's eyes are clear and open.

76

76. *The Suffering Black Madonna* (Acrylic on canvas,
Autumn 1983)

CHAPTER 8

Transformations

Transformations is a series of forty charcoal drawings done between July 4, 1987, and February 4, 1988.

77

77. The woman feels that she cannot go on. For endless years she has journeyed along that inner wall which cuts her off from life, always hoping that at some time a door to a more bearable existence would open up. She grew up violated, mistreated, living in constant fear, with no one to turn to. She could not protect herself and no one paid attention to the realities of her life or even looked at her. Now she is stuck with the results of the abuse and her own hopelessness. At the same time she is aware that things could be far worse, and that there are many people out there who are crying with her.

78

80

81

79

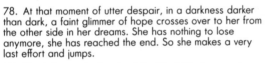

78. At that moment of utter despair, in a darkness darker than dark, a faint glimmer of hope crosses over to her from the other side in her dreams. She has nothing to lose anymore, she has reached the end. So she makes a very last effort and jumps.

79. She falls into the hands of the Black Madonna, who has been waiting for her in the background, all the time watching her struggles, her afflictions, her quest, testing her character, adding to her substance, comforting her in mysterious dreams, and expecting her to cross over.

80. Now they have found each other. They look each other in the eyes, they size each other up, they like what they see. As they begin to understand what has really happened, they decide to play together for a long time.

81. The woman has a great unmet need to be mothered and cared for. Therefore, the first thing that the Black Madonna does is take the woman in and feed her tenderly as she feeds all life (Dream No. 21).

82

83

84

82. She even makes a nest in Her hair in which the woman can rest, heal, and dream. She supports her and cares for her lovingly, as She supports and cares for all beings on the planet (Active Imagination No. 29).

83. A blooming tree grows out of the healing pool in the inner sanctum of the woman's soul. This is the place where the Black Madonna dwells and where She can be met (Dream No. 41).

84. Four rivers flow from that black pool, and the Black Madonna's hands have become the firm ground under the woman's feet (Dream No. 31).

85

86

87

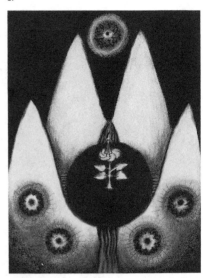

88

85. The woman delights in contemplating the Black Madonna. She stands at the rim of that healing spring with her animals, just gazing in amazement, as the four rivers carry crystal clear water from the black depth to the mountains.

86. The wheel of life turns fast, but the Black Madonna, standing in the center, is the still space within the woman's heart.

87. The Black Madonna is the woman's great find. She is her beloved "jewel in the lotus."

88. The roots of the lotus flower reach deep and far into the earth. They are ancient pipelines of energy, coming out of unfathomable depths. They always were and always will be.

89

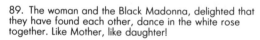

90

91

89. The woman and the Black Madonna, delighted that they have found each other, dance in the white rose together. Like Mother, like daughter!

90. How patient and loving the Black Madonna is: She lets the woman do her own thing and take her own sweet time.

91. In the meantime the Black Madonna has lit the Sabbath lights and set the table, which is her altar (Dream No. 21).

92

92. She blesses the wine (Dream No. 21).

93

94

96

95

93. Her cup overflows towards the people.

94. Rivers of grace stream in abundance from the black chalice.

95. Sun and moon have united (Dreams Nos. 1 and 36).

96. The woman does a labor of pure love: she combs and brushes the Mother's hair.

97

97. Then the Black Madonna takes care of the woman's
hair until it shines.

98

99

100

101

102

98. The Black Madonna and the woman contemplate each other's faces under the stars. The Mother rocks Her child gently and tells Her a story.

99. And then the woman witnesses the Mass of the Black Madonna (Dreams Nos. 11 and 21).

100. The woman receives a light that shines in the darkness: Light of Light.

101. The woman has become a vessel of living light.

102. She looks into the mirror and discovers her dark sister. That is, she becomes conscious of her shadow side.

103

104

105

103. The sisters come from the same mother, and have found each other again in the heart space of the Black Madonna.

104. They do inner work together until their vessels are filled and overflow.

105. The woman has dreamt that the wheat of her own vessel streamed into the vessel of her black sister and simultaneously vice versa. In the dream a voice called this process the Reconciliation. And now the woman realizes that what the dream showed as a possibility is now really taking place in her own depths as well as in outer life.

106

107

108

106. So the women go to the mirror together, where each woman recognizes herself in the other.

107. Four women now take Holy Communion together by eating the Mother's body.

108. The earth has become the woman's destiny. She finds her stars in the soil.

109

110

111

112

113

109. Like all beings, the sisters are part of the web of life.

110. They stand together with one foot in this world and one in the other.

111. They have bonded together in a sisterhood.

112. They have built an earth altar inside a tree and lit the candles. In the silence of their contemplation a white rose blooms.

113. The women have prepared a meal for each other in their own house. They take communion together.

114

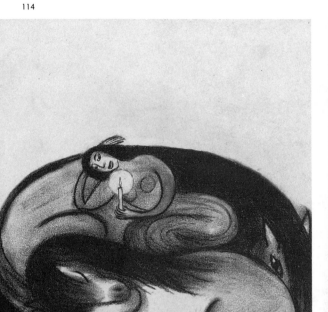

115

114. Having found the Black Madonna and her sisters, the woman is content. She has overcome the wall and crossed over into the fullness of life. And so she rests among the animals with open eyes, holding the light close to her heart.

115. No wall separates her from life anymore.

116

116. Having found peace and serenity within, she has
come into her own.

CHAPTER 9

The Great Mother with Lovers in Her Hair

I drew this picture of the Black Madonna as the Great Mother of all Life seven years after I had experienced the image in active imagination (Active Imagination No. 29). She lovingly nourishes all beings with Her own substance. The two lovers, who are so comfortable in Her hair, as if they are lying in a nest, are Her Crown. The closer one holds on to Her, the deeper the delight in life.

As the stars dance around Her, She rests self-contained in the center.

117

117. *The Great Mother with Lovers in Her Hair* (Charcoal drawing, August 30, 1988)

The Hands of the Black Madonna the Creator

I have dreamt several times about the lovely big hands of the Black Madonna. One of the dreams is included in this book (Dream No. 31). While I drew the picture, I contemplated Her Hands from which life springs and eternally renews itself. We all have come from this source. The Earth makes people, plants, and animals just like a tree makes leaves. And some day we will all return to Her. It is good to remember death as a part of life, because that drives home the fact that we cannot afford to lose time, that we have only each other, that we all are linked together by a common fate and desperately need each other, and that *this is it!* This life is the only life we have, and there is no other life more eternal or more sacred. These thoughts occupied my mind as my hands made the picture.

118. *The Hands of the Black Madonna the Creator*
(Charcoal drawing, August 31, 1988)

118

CHAPTER 11

The Passion and Redemption of the Black Madonna

he Passion and Redemption of the Black Madonna is a series of twenty-seven charcoal drawings done between April 10, 1988, and March 12, 1989.

119

119. Her Hidden Face.

120

120. I saw Her imprisoned in a dungeon underneath the
city of Chicago. She was tied up, had been horribly
tortured, and was kneeling in Her own hot tears. She cried
out: "Behold and see if there be any sorrow like unto My
sorrow!" Only the rocks wept for Her.

121

121. She is despised and rejected, a Woman of Sorrows.
No one sees Her, no one hears Her. She suffers endlessly
in silence.

122

122. She looks for someone to have pity on Her, but there
is no one.

123

124

125

123. Boxed in, cut off from the land of the living, she drinks her own tears. Torment beyond endurance has driven Her to the edge of madness.

124. Ice age of the soul! She has been frozen out of our lives. I hear Her cry: "Have pity on me! Have pity on me!"

125. "My God, my God, why hast Thou forsaken me?"

126

126. The little girl has been crucified in an ice cube. Her starved body weeps helpless tears. The Earth herself screams in protest against the crime of soul murder. A rod, a crown of thorns, and the sponge with vinegar speak of the physical, mental, and emotional tortures which the child had to endure and which have left their stigmata on her body.

127. Consciousness journeying inward is the only ray of hope.

128. The woman has found a way to the underground realm of the Black Madonna with the help of her dreams and active imaginations. She stays with the Black Madonna and weeps and grieves with Her (Active Imagination No. 44). At the same time she keeps her eyes open as she holds the light and her obsidian knife firmly in her hands, ready to use them as soon as she possibly can.

129. The woman has cut the Black Madonna from the whipping post. The Mother is still sobbing and Her face is wet with tears. The woman uses her shaman's drum to comfort the Mother and to heal the pain in Her Heart. She has lit sage and cedar in her abalone shell and smudges and cleanses the dungeon. The sweet smell of the smoke refreshes the Mother and the human warmth brings hope to the frozen infant.

127

128

129

130

131

132

130. Lightning and thunder add huge amounts of energy to the small fire in the abalone shell (Dream No. 8). And so the thawing out process takes its course. The woman and the Black Madonna work together as equals to save, heal, and nurture the child. This work is utter joy.

131. A lightning bolt has changed the whipping post into a column of the finest, clearest rock crystal, and the torture chamber into a sacred place of transformation deep in the earth, hidden from view. Bonded in their love for the child, the Mother and the woman gladly acknowledge their equality.

132. How the dungeon has changed. Not only is it a stable now, where they all lovingly take care of each other, but it is filled with tremendous energy from the crystal column which builds and builds. The Mother has used Her snowy veil to make a soft little nest for Her little girl. And look at her now!

133

134

133. How the child has grown! Together with the woman
she is at home in the lap of the Black Madonna and
dances to the sound of the woman's dream rattle, filled
with live seeds from the fields.

134. In Her underground Sanctuary the Black Madonna
blesses the world with the Holy of Holies, Her Heart in the
golden monstrance. And the woman with the child rests in
Her hair as comfortably as in a nest (Active Imagination
No. 29).

135

135. In the meantime the woman has dreamt several times about the Native American White Buffalo Woman holding the Sacred Pipe. White Buffalo Woman has come from the prairies of the Holy Land to the big city to visit with the Black Madonna, the woman, and the child and to dance with them to the heartbeat of Mother Earth.

136

136. The Goddesses meet as equals in the chapel underneath Chicago. Each has brought with Her the riches of Her native soil. The vessels of the Black Madonna are filled to the brim with European clover honey and wheat.

The vessels of White Buffalo Woman overflow with wildflower honey from the prairies of the United States and corn. Two cottonwood branches carry white roses.

137

138

139

140

137. They have mixed corn, wheat, and honey and baked a rich, nourishing bread together. They have filled the cup with water from the inner well. And they have invited all the animals to the round table for the meal. As they eat together, a new Covenant of Love is born.

138. The Black Madonna and White Buffalo Woman now plan an initiation ceremony for the woman. In preparing for it the Black Madonna holds the stars from the woman's dream of the conjunction in Her hands (Dream No. 36). White Buffalo Woman, on the other hand, has joined all the dream animals into a column, the woman's personal totem pole.

139. Protected and supported by the Goddesses, the woman thus witnesses the union of her European spiritual heritage and of her new life on North American soil: the stars merge with the animals in her body. From now on she will carry her light and two white roses in one hand, and the pipe bag with her sacred pipe in the other.

140. Suddenly the earth has split open in the shape of an even-armed cross and the woman witnesses the ascension of the Black Madonna into the light of day (Active Imagination No. 44).

141

142

141. She escapes from underneath Chicago with the cry: "Free at last! Free at last! Thank God I am free at last!"

142. I see them over there against the summer sky. They are all there: White Buffalo Woman, the Black Madonna, the woman, the child, the red rainbow-hued bird from above, the blue-green owl, the golden eagle, the deer, the little black horse, the buffalo, the cat, and the Black Bear (Dreams Nos. 13 and 16). The Sacred Pipe invites them to dance. And so they dance away from the big city and it is a sacred dance towards the blooming prairies of the Holy Land. And how glad they are to have each other! (Since the age of nineteen or so I have loved Ingmar Bergman's film *The Seventh Seal*. It was a helpful mirror of the human condition for me and ended with a "dance of Death." In this picture I painted my own "dance of Life.")

143

145

143. White Buffalo Woman takes them all into Her Sanctuary, which is the Golden Tipi of Reconciliation (Active Imagination No. 45). There they sit comfortably around the fire and watch the smoke from the Sacred Pipe, which lets them see their own breath and proves to them that all beings are relatives.

144. See facing page.

145. This is the *Earth Cathedral* (Dreams Nos. 5, 26, and 35). The doors are wide open. The tree, which grows out of the healing waters, stands in bloom (Dream No. 41). People of all colors, races, creeds, and nationalities meet in a circle to reconcile, to celebrate their interconnectedness with all life on the planet, and to commit themselves to heal and save the suffering Earth.

144

144. This is the *Monstrance of the Black Madonna*. It is the
tree of life, the Cosmos itself. The *Holy of Holies* floating
right in the middle of it is our planet Earth, the most
precious fruit of the Universe. There! I hear White Buffalo
Woman singing: "Earth, she is our mother, behold Her,
most beautiful and most sacred."

CHAPTER 12

Gifts and Blessings

G ifts and Blessings is a series of four charcoal drawings done between May 19 and June 2, 1989.

146

146. In her active imaginations the woman saw the Earth radiant with an inner light and not at all lost in space, but watched over by powers that greatly care about her fate.

147

147. She saw the Black Madonna, White Buffalo Woman,
the Kwan Yin, and the Shekinah come from the four
directions. They stood on golden clouds, watching over the
Earth (Active Imagination No. 47).

148

149

148. The Goddesses knelt down around the planet. While the Earth hovered in the center, they created a sacred energy field around it with their hands. The pure love streaming from one Divine Heart to the next then formed a second invisible energy field around the first one, sending love and comfort to all beings on the planet. And they blessed and healed the suffering Earth.

149. The Goddesses brought four gifts for the people. The gift of the Black Madonna is Her Golden Monstrance, in which She holds up the Earth for adoration. White Buffalo Woman brought Her Sacred Pipe to make visible the breath that all beings on the planet share and to convince everyone of the interdependence of all life forms. The Kwan Yin left Her lotus flower, Her white rose, which speaks of the pure space within the heart, seat of generosity, understanding, and compassion for all beings. And the Shekinah brought Her twin candles, the shining lights of consciousness and clarity of mind. These sacred lights call us to draw strength and inspiration from that inexhaustible well deep within our souls, so that we may evolve as persons of real presence and quality, aware of our responsibilities and moral obligations to the Earth. They call us to cultivate wisdom, ingenuity, and initiative, and to live and work with intensity and conviction for the sake of our beloved home planet and all its inhabitants.

CHAPTER 13

In the Sanctuary of the Black Madonna

I*n the Sanctuary of the Black Madonna* is a series of five charcoal drawings done between October 1 and October 15, 1989.

151

152

150. See Overleaf.

151. A lovely black cloud about which the woman once dreamt hovers in the chapel. It opens up and reveals the Golden Cloud of the Goddesses, who are carrying the Daughter of the Earth.

152. Out of this mystery the Christ Child is born and she is a little Black Madonna (Dream No. 50). The woman reverently kneels down before Her on the bearskin, surrounded by the gifts of the Goddesses which have become essential components of her life.

150

150. The woman carries the Chapel of the Black Madonna
in her heart (Dream No. 9). It is an inner space into which
she retreats to do her inner work. Every detail of this
sanctuary has appeared in her dreams. The woman
incubates dreams and does active imagination on the black
bearskin.

153

153. This is the Host of the Black Madonna. It is the
Sacred Earth, which the North American Indians call Turtle
Island. The Earth holds the Divine Child in its center with all
the animals around it. The woman is an integral part of it
all. She kneels before the monstrance in adoration and
uses her drum for healing.

154

154. The woman takes Holy Communion from the hands of
the Black Madonna and receives a vision of Her
Assumption.

CHAPTER 14

Missa Nigrae Virginis (Mass of the Black Virgin)

On January 19, 1990, I dreamt that I held an earth-ball, a globe of the world, in both hands and was saying the Mass of the Black Madonna over it. I then made the pictures and wrote the words down. Following the pattern of my inner growth the text changed over the years. I wrote this version in the spring of 1993.

155

155. VENITE ADOREMUS SANCTAM TERRAM (COME LET US ADORE THE SACRED EARTH)—Come, my brothers and sisters, let us celebrate the numinous mysterium of our inner world. Let us meet in the Earth Cathedral to honor Nature within and without. Let us spend time with the Black Madonna, so that She can be a mother to us and help us.

156

156. INTROIBO AD ALTARE TERRAE (I WILL GO IN UNTO THE ALTAR OF THE EARTH)—I will go to the altar of the Great Mystery within and kneel before the Tree of Life. Brothers and sisters, can you see the transcendent beauty of the world, the Mind inside Nature, the Mother, who wants to be honored and loved? She has filled me with joy since my youth.

157

157. CONFITEOR DOMINAE (I CONFESS TO THE DIVINE LADY)—And still I must confess to you, Mother, and to you brothers and sisters that I have sinned against Life and Nature many times. Show me your Light and your Truth, that they may cleanse me and draw me to you. O Loving One, sustain me, that I do not shirk my responsibilities towards You and the inner work demanded of me. Show me the way and speak to me in dreams for the sake of the planet and all beings. Great Mystery, protect the Earth in the Still Space of Your Heart and save us all.

GLORIA TERRAE (GLORY BE TO THE EARTH)—Glory be to the Great Mystery in us and peace to all men and women of good will. Brothers and sisters, let us adore the Epiphany of the Infinite in the flow of this transitory life. Let us embrace the Earth. Let us delight in all livings things, cherish and bless them. Come, let us immerse ourselves in the abundance of Nature within and without for the healing and renewal of our souls and the world.

158   159

158. CREDO IN UNAM TERRAM, SANCTAM MATREM
NOSTRAM (I BELIEVE IN ONE EARTH OUR HOLY
MOTHER)—I believe in the inner mystery of the world, the
Mother, who connects us all. From Her we come and to
Her we will return. Nurtured by Her body and carried by
Her through the immensity of space and time, we are Her
sons and daughters. We are linked to each other, to our
ancestors, to our children and children's children, and to all
living beings on the planet as relatives. All of us together
are like one extended family. Therefore, brothers and
sisters, let us look out for each other and get to know one
another, so that we may come together into a community
of the spirit to devote ourselves to the mystery living within
everyone of us and to take care of the Earth in her great
suffering and sorrow. The Mother desperately needs our
help and waits for us to join together in a spiritual network
for the healing of the planet in these complex and troubled
times.

SANCTA, SANCTA, SANCTA DOMINA MATER TERRA
(HOLY, HOLY, HOLY, DIVINE LADY MOTHER EARTH)—Holy,
holy, holy is the Earth. Contained in her is the numinous
Mysterium of Life. Loving Nature within ourselves we will
find the Mother, saving Nature without we will flourish.
Holding the Mother sacred we will be sanctified.

159. HOC EST ENIM CORPUS MEUM (FOR THIS IS MY
BODY)—The Mother feeds and waters us all the time. She
says to us: "This is my body, the stuff of Life, take it and
eat it, all of you!" Every day of our lives we live off Her.
Does Nature not sustain and nourish us with Herself? Is She
not generous? Brothers and sisters, where then does the
Earth end and we begin? Are we not one body and soul
with Her? Are we not all breathing the same air and
drinking the same water? Are we not like all the other
beings on the planet and related to them in pleasure and in
pain, in joy and in sorrow? We are the Earth! The Divine
Mind inside nature is our own deepest Self and has
brought us forth. We, the people, are the carriers of
consciousness. And therefore we are accountable: we are
our Mother's keepers; there is no one else who can or will
look out for Her. Should the Earth perish, all living things
must go down with Her, because She is the great mother
body that carries us all and we have no other home in the
Universe. Her suffering is great. Everyone of us is
responsible for Her in his or her own place and must work
according to his or her capabilities to help save the
Mother. We cannot afford to waste anymore time. Let us
therefore go to the Black Madonna and ask for dreams of
guidance to learn what needs to be done. The Loving One
will hear us and answer us in Her own language. She will
send us the dreams because She needs us badly. She who
protects, nurtures, and blesses us so abundantly, cannot
help Herself and cries out to us to protect, nurture, and
bless Her in return by doing the necessary inner and outer
work to save the planet.

160   161

160. MANDATUM NOVUM DO VOBIS: TENETE TERRAM CARAM (I GIVE YOU A NEW COMMANDMENT: LOVE THE EARTH)—I dreamt of a new Commandment: Love the Earth with your whole heart, with your whole soul, with your whole mind, and with your whole strength! Brothers and sisters, we belong irrevocably to the Earth. We have no life and no future apart from her. Our fate is tied to the fate of the planet and we are all together in this. Therefore let us love one another, be with each other, care for one another and for all living beings: for the peoples of all colors, races, genders, creeds, and nationalities, for the children and the elders, for the sick and the healthy, for the poor and the rich, for the weak and the strong, for the animals, the trees and plants, for the fields and prairies, the mountains and deserts, the air, the rivers, the lakes, the oceans, and all living things. We all need each other. Everyone matters, everyone counts. Each one of us is vulnerable, but each one also has gifts to give. Brothers and sisters, do you see the innocence, the stupendous

beauty, and the appalling defenselessness of Nature? Let us gladly acknowledge our interdependence, delight in it, and accept the responsibilities which come with it. Let us tune in to the Great Mystery in our own depths to come together on the inner plane and under the direction and protection of the Mother, let us take care of the world. The Mother will speak to us in dreams and visions and tell us what to do. She will reveal her needs to us and teach us how to become guardian angels of the planet. She will join us together into a spiritual network to balance the Earth from within.

161. MATER NOSTRA, QUAE ES TERRA (OUR MOTHER WHO ART THE EARTH)—Our Mother, you who are the Light of Nature and the numinous mysterium of the inner world, hallowed be Thy name. Bless us and help us to do Your great work: to stand up for the planet, the people, and all living things.

162

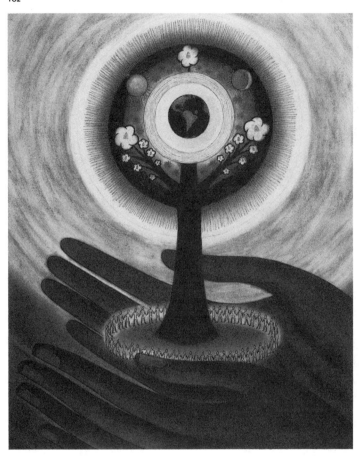

162. ITE MISSA EST (GO, THE MASS HAS ENDED)—Dear
brothers and sisters, as we go forth now to do our work,
may a deep and abiding love for our home planet flame in
our hearts and link up with the love in the hearts of those
people all over the world, who are called by the Mother to
save the Earth. Her Holy Spirit will leap from heart to heart
and surround the planet with a mantle of healing energy
through us. This vocation of self giving will be the golden
thread that knots our souls together on the inner level into
a spiritual safety net for the world.

   Brothers and sisters, let us devote ourselves to the
required inner work for the sake of our souls as well as for
the sake of the planet and the living things. Thus we will
gather around the Great Mystery, all of us standing on
solid ground inside ourselves, on that patch of inner
eternity which not even death can touch. The Mother will
guide us. She will talk in dreams to each and every one of
us from within our souls to comfort, inspire, and strengthen
us. We are Her only hope. Because we want to console
and heal her, She will respond and water us from our own
inner well and fill us with Her mysteries.

                    A M E N

CHAPTER 15

My Personal Myth

The decisive question for man is: Is he related to something infinite or not? That is the telling question of his life. Only if we know that the thing which truly matters is the infinite can we avoid fixing our interest upon futilities, and upon all kinds of goals which are not of real importance. . . . If we understand and feel that here in this life we already have a link with the infinite, desires and attitudes change. In the final analysis, we count for something only because of the essential we embody, and if we do not embody that, life is wasted.

—C. G. JUNG
Memories, Dreams, Reflections[1]

Twenty years ago, I came across a book by C. G. Jung for the first time in my life. It was called *Man and his Symbols* and contained many pictures. It also included chapters by several other leading Jungian thinkers. The book in my hands opened to the chapter on the individuation process by Marie-Louise von Franz.

I remember looking at the first two illustrations of that chapter which show a "meander" and a detail of the same meander. I read that all the dreams of a person in the course of his or her whole life seen together are parts of "one great web" and create "a meandering pattern in which individual strands or tendencies become visible, then vanish, then return again."[2]

At that time I did not dream and knew absolutely nothing about my own unconscious inner life. But contemplating the small fragment of that meander, which illustrates a single dream, and then the whole meander, which stands for the "total dream life of the individual," I felt such a mysterious and inexplicable longing to know my own depths and to find the pattern of my destiny, that it almost hurt. When I read on that the deepest part of our soul, the Self, "can be defined as an inner guiding factor that is different from the conscious personality and that can be grasped only through the investigation of one's own dreams," my curiosity was aroused. What I was reading was so interesting that on the spot I made up my mind to check this out and to conduct my own experiment with the unconscious. On that day I began to do inner work.

It has taken me twenty years of intense and persistent effort to get a clear feeling for my own meander, that is, for the blueprint of my existence. I have no name for what drives me to devote so much time and energy to soul making. I go by intuition, convinced that this work is of supreme importance for my life and well-being.

Looking at my evergrowing pattern I see in its center my very first dream. More and more this childhood dream reveals itself to me as a virgin spring coming out of unfathomable depths. All my other dreams and all my pictures are somehow connected to it. Nowadays I find myself contemplating that dream time and again because it spoke to me so early and so eloquently about my destiny and the essence of my life.

I have always been moved by the first sentence of C. G. Jung's autobiography: "My life is a story of the self-realization of the unconscious."[3] It gives me a deep feeling of kinship because I recognize a similar fate happening to me. My childhood dream already spelled it out. But I had to carry that dream for almost half a century in my heart and in my whole being before I could decipher its severe symbolism and know that this dream was a first encounter with the transpersonal psyche, the Self.

The dream came to me at the age of three and a half years in the midst of traumatic experiences and extreme loneliness. It said to me: "Fear not. You are protected and will not be destroyed. No matter what sufferings and deaths life has in store for you, you will survive. In the deepest darkness imaginable, where no one wants to go, you will find the light. You matter, you count. Take heart and trust the life force in your own inner depth, because that is where your true home is. There you will find safety and do your life's work." That is how I understand the dream today. But when it came, it expressed itself, of course, through the vocabulary of the Catholic religion in which I was being raised, that is, in the traditional concepts of Heaven and Hell, God and the Devil, Redemption and Damnation, Divine Light in the sky and Hellfire in the Earth.

The dream scared me very much, because I took it literally as I did not know that dreams speak in symbols and metaphors. I had no way to find out that "Heaven and hell are the two aspects of transpersonal libido."[4] And of course I never suspected that others before me had dreamt similar dreams and spent a lifetime working out the meaning, for instance, C. G. Jung[5] and a dreamer referred to by Marie-Louise von Franz.[6] "Childhood is a period of great emotional intensity, and a child's earliest dreams often manifest in symbolic form the basic structure of the psyche, indicating how it will later shape the destiny of the individual concerned."[7]

This is the dream as recorded many years ago. It repeated itself again and again.

1942–1945

I dreamt that I had died and come into the presence of God. I trembled with fear because this was the moment which would decide my fate for all eternity.

God was present in a great white light in the sky. This light was all-knowing, cold, and silent. Without words he condemned me to eternal Hell.

Unspeakable dread filled me, as I fell backwards into a dark hole in the ground. For an endless time I fell vertically through a black tunnel and finally landed on my feet in Hell. Hell was a fiery cave deep inside of the earth.

My terror grew because I had to walk through the flames. I saw to my left several small chambers filled with fire where people were suffering the torments of Hell.

Under no circumstances did I want to share their fate. I searched feverishly in my mind for a way out, although I knew well there was none. Suddenly I had an idea. What, if I would offer myself as a servant to the Devil? Surely he needed someone to sweep and clean his house, do his laundry, carry his water, bake his bread, and cook his meals. If I could show him that I was good at all this, maybe he would soften towards me. Maybe he would even treat me well in exchange for work well done.

Barely had I thought all this when the Devil entered from the right. He did not look at all like in the pictures. He was a huge, terrifying presence, reaching from floor to ceiling, like a column of living fire. He looked at me. With shaking voice I asked him, if I could be his maidservant. Without hesitation he said, "Yes."

My terror changed to bliss. In the worst of all possible places I had found safety. From now on I worked for the Devil. I cooked and fried his food in black sooty pots and pans over the Hellfire, which burned strongly in an old brick hearth.

Hell was filled with warmth and light from the fire, and the flames around me did not burn me.

When I look at that dream today, I am astounded and ask myself, what is that mysterious force within the depth of a human being which creates such a dream? Did it not come at a crucial time in my life, not to frighten but to console and guide me when I felt abandoned by God and humankind, and when my very existence was threatened? Soon I would have to face the possibility of physical death on a daily basis and would find myself in other perilous and insoluble situations. This dream contains the essence of my life in a nutshell. I would like to describe how I learned in the course of many years and with great effort to interpret this dream and to love it. Because I now understand that the dream was my first shamanic journey, a first descent into the unconscious which is that space deep within me from which decades later the dreams about the Black Madonna would arise. At the time when I dreamt it I had no one and nowhere to turn to for help in the outside world. But the dream, although I did not comprehend it at the time, promised me a way out. It said that through inner work and sheer intensity I would be able to transcend my suffering, discover its meaning, and turn it into rapture. Over the years I have often felt offended by the dream as I wrestled with its weird and "negative" vocabulary. But I took courage from the work of C. G. Jung who wrote that "a glance at the Scriptures . . . is enough to show us the importance of the devil in the divine drama of redemption."[8]

I would like to tell something about the circumstances in which the little dreamer found herself, how she felt, and how she experienced life in rural Germany in 1942. She had been born in Berlin half a year before the outbreak of World War II in 1939 and was brought to her maternal grandmother's home in the country because of the air raids on the capital.

That three-and-a-half-year-old child stands so clearly before my inner eyes and in my heart. I see how shy she is, how very sad and abandoned. She does not understand why she is being scolded and whipped so often and locked into a dark room for punishment. She is hurting badly, but no one speaks to her or helps her. She weeps and cries out to God and the angels. But God is silent as ever and never answers or stops her tormentors. She folds her hands, she makes the sign of the cross, she calls for the Blessed Mother. But no one answers, no one comes. There is only silence, deadly, inescapable silence, and the pain.

During the night she dreams that she is dying and that she is dead. And in the dream she knows that her eternal fate is about to be decided. Judgment Day, with which Grandmother threatens her so often, has dawned for her. And so she comes into the presence of the all-good, all-just, and all-powerful God, who lives in a brilliant white light in the sky. Still, God is silent as ever. Surely He knows her because He knows everything. But He agrees with her family that she does not belong in Heaven, that she does not deserve to be forever happy with Him, that she needs to be punished and excluded from the community of the saints. And without saying even one word to her, ruling her with His glance alone like her mother does, He condemns her to burn for all eternity in Hell.

The little girl had dreaded this moment. Shaking with fear she had hoped against all hope, as only children can do, to be allowed to go to Heaven too. And now that it is all decided she does not protest. God's utter cruelty appears to her as justice, because for that little girl, who did not know anything else, the silence of God and the injustices of humanity were the basic experiences of her life.

But to comprehend her world fully, one needs to know that her life was also blessed with two sources of pure joy. One of them was her grandmother's vegetable, fruit, and flower garden. There she experienced the Radiance of the Earth and the comforting cycles of the seasons. The other was a huge old fashioned hearth in the kitchen. Her grandfather, who was a master brick mason and worked most of the time in the surrounding villages, had built it with his own hands from smooth red bricks. The hearth contained not only one, but two firespots. He had modernized an old Pomeranian Black Kitchen and transformed it into a comfortable working place for his wife and six daughters.[9] There Grandmother did her wonderful cooking, frying, baking, and canning over the live wood and coal fires. On dark evenings the child was allowed to sit on a footstool before an open hearth door to look into the fire and watch the sparks fall through the grill into the ashes. And with a small paring knife she would cut slivers from a fragrant piece of resinous pinewood to make kindling for the next day.

Grandmother was a tall, slim woman with ill-fitting dentures that fell out when she scolded me and a thin braid coiled into a bun at the back of her head. Although in her seventies, she had raven-black hair and blue eyes. Spent from raising a big family, careworn from having suffered through three wars, overworked, sad, silent, and often sick, she never smiled at the child or took her into her arms. Going to mass daily was her only respite. Her lips used to move in silent prayer as she went about her never-ending work in the house, root cellar, outdoor pantry, chicken coop, wash shed, and garden. Often she fed me two sugar cubes with drops of Valerian (a sedative) in them. She always wore black because her favorite daughter, my godmother, had died shortly after I arrived. The house was old. It had no plumbing, except for a single water faucet in the kitchen underneath which a zinc pail stood in place of a drain to catch the drips. I remember how in the spring Grandmother used to carry manure into her garden by using a rusty bucket fastened to a stick, which she filled from the smelly pit underneath the outhouse on the other side of the chicken coop.

I was brought to Grandmother's home at the age of one and a half and lived with her there for seven years until we were forcibly relocated after the end of World War II and the house and land were taken away from us. The first thing she did when I came was tie a bundle of birch branches together with a piece of string and hang it over the kitchen door. That was *the rod*. It could be seen from every angle of the kitchen, which served as the main living area, to remind the little girl that the dear God saw everything she did and that there was no place to hide from His glance. That rod was a source of unspeakable anguish for the child. Grandmother needed only to briefly look up to it or nod in its direction to make the child totally submissive. She had learned at that early age that anyone can be broken and made to do anything if enough pain is inflicted.

The rod was used to "break her will" as the adults always said. When they wanted to punish her, they first made preparations by setting up a chair for Grandmother or Mother to sit down on and by showing her the rod. Then the child, after having had her skirt lifted over her head and her pants pulled down, was placed across the adult's knees with head hanging down on one side and legs on the other and was held in place. Then she was beaten hard with the rod on her bare bottom. This was considered a necessary and effective lesson in obedience. After that came the moral lesson. The child had to stand straight, receive the rod from Grandmother's hands, hold it up before her eyes, look at it, and thank it for the pain with a prayer: *"Liebe Rut', mach mich gut, mach mich fromm, dass ich in den Himmel komm!"* (Translated this means: Dear rod, make me good, make me pious, so that I can be sure to go to Heaven.) She had to say the prayer loud and clear, and if she had not succeeded by now in swallowing her tears and was still sobbing, she was hit until the crying stopped. If she stuttered she had to repeat the prayer. For a long time afterwards the child could not sit without great pain but was made to do so anyway. She was told to offer up all difficulties to Jesus. Many times the adults told her that they punished her only out of love for her salvation and for her own good. Nothing in life really mattered except to go to Heaven when death came, and since no one knew the hour, one had to be prepared at all times. Each night they all prayed for a good death. Her mother told her many times how much sadness the little girl caused her by forcing her hands: "If you only knew how much I suffer when I have to punish you . . . It hurts me more than it could possibly ever hurt you." The basic emotions in the child's life were fear and shame. She has no memories of love, of hugs and kisses, of gifts, or simply being together in trust. Even today the pain of my inner child is so great that I do not dare to go into the emotions.

For most of my life I thought that being treated with such cruelty was an exception until I came across the work of Morton Schatzman, who has researched the German tradition of disciplining children into total obedience.[10] I understood then that my grandmother and mother did to me what had been done to them as children. Ingmar Bergman's film, *Fanny and Alexander,* helped me even more because it presents this so-called "strong and harsh love" visually. In the child Alexander, who is beaten by the bishop and lectured on truth and love, I see myself. But only recently, when I found a book on the history of corporal punishment, did I become aware of how many human beings all over the world suffered and still suffer the same fate.[11]

Tataya was raised like generations of other children in families of the Catholic clergy. I can confirm from my own experiences Eugen Drewermann's research. He is a German psychoanalyst and Catholic priest who has written about the problems of people who have grown up in families of the clergy, that is, in families which count a priest or a nun among their members.[12] In my parent's generation alone there were nine clerics, namely my mother's four sisters who all joined the same order and on my father's side two of his ten siblings, one of whom became a missionary priest in Africa, and three of his maternal first cousins. My father himself had been shaped by years in the seminary just like his own father before him and my mother often expressed her regret over not having followed her sisters into the cloister. I grew up surrounded by Catholic clerics and in their atmosphere felt almost as if I were living in a convent. Their tradition of making children blindly obedient for their own good was deeply ingrained in my family for generations. The members of my family looked, moved, talked, thought, acted and behaved very much like the bishop, his mother, sister, and servants in Ingmar Bergman's film *Fanny and Alexander*.

The utter lovelessness of that environment froze the child's vulnerable soul and would have destroyed her had it not been for the dream, the fire in her grandmother's hearth, and the garden. Nature became Tataya's refuge. The garden nurtured her tender heart in the same way that the fire in the hearth warmed her and the dream explained her destiny to her.

I remember her standing barefoot on the warm soil under a large cherry tree in full bloom, and how she felt surrounded on all sides by the gentle light and fragrance of the snowy blossoms. They had miraculously come out of that old tree which was so safely rooted in the good black earth. With all her senses she drank into herself this sacred radiance of the Earth.

Everything in the garden became her beloved friend because the garden was filled with supernal beauty. She let the beetles with their iridescent green wings climb up her fingers so that they could take off from the tips. She cupped her little hands around the flowers to feel them opening up against her palms and breathed on them so they would not forget to make their petals shine in all colors of the rainbow for her. Sunlight would stream through translucent golden-green gooseberries and red currants and make them glow. And the starlings got into the habit of taking care of her by throwing the sweetest cherries from the treetop down to her with a peck of their beaks.

I still remember the delicious taste of those black shrivelled up cherries out of which the birds had taken a bite. The little girl picked them up, blew the dust off, and ate them one by one while kneeling on the ground and pulling weeds in the summer heat.

But best of all she liked autumn, when the trees changed color and the blue plums were gathered. She was taught to take their pits out of the yellow inside with the round end of one of her grandmother's hairpins and to crack them with a stone. They tasted like bitter almonds. Oh, how she loved the smell of smoke in the cold air when Grandmother burned the potato weeds in late fall! And the fragrance of big, sweet, homegrown apples baking in the oven made her heart glad as she watched the snowflakes drifting down by the kitchen window and icicles glittering in the winter light.

I see her so eager for life and so innocent.

And I could weep when I picture this little three-and-a-half-year-old child being informed about Hell and Eternal Damnation. She is being told that this is where God will send her because she is depraved and unfit for life. She had been violated by a priest and then by her father. Grandmother and Mother blame her for it and try to "drive the Devil out of her" with the rod. I see her lying on her back in bed in the evening, very still and with arms crossed high over her chest. Her mother stands by the statue of the Sacred Heart of Jesus, rod in hand, watching that the little girl does not move and that she goes to sleep in this stiff position.

And she is so very scared. She is afraid of everyone and everything, even afraid to go to sleep, because then the dream will come again, that terrible dream which seals her fate. There is no one she can turn to, no one who will help her. The adults know what has been done to her, but they believe her tormentors who are lying to save face. She is only three and a half years old but so "bad" that she is not even allowed to play with her only playmate, her two-year-old sister.

Finally she falls asleep and there comes the dream again: even God rejects her for all eternity. He condemns her to go to Hell. She feels pushed and falls backwards into that deep black hole in the ground and through the endless dark tunnel. It takes forever, but she lands upright on her feet in that dreaded place.

Nowadays I sometimes talk to that little girl in my heart and tell her that shamans all over the world have dreams like hers. Since time immemorial the shamanic tradition has reported similar visions. Shamans journey in their dreams and trances through a black tunnel into the visionary realm of the underworld. And they call this inner place the womb of Mother Earth. There they confront spirits, are tried by fire, and have to come to terms with the life energy force,[13] exactly like little Tataya in her dream.

I tell her how the Christian belief system into which she was born did not recognize shamanic experiences and had no words for them when they occurred. I tell her that she could not have guessed that the inner space to which she journeyed was really the realm of the Black Madonna where she could walk safely through the fire and find a home. And that the dream was a good thing for her.

The inner space called Hell (*Hoelle* in my native German) is synonymous with the

Underworld of dreams and visions during shamanic experiences and with the Unconscious of modern depth psychology. The word 'Hell' is derived from the name of the pre-Christian Goddess Hel, the Earth Mother. My European ancestors believed that she welcomed the souls of the departed into her lap.[14] A remnant of her has survived in old fairytales as *Frau Holle* and the Devil's Great Grandmother. The English word "Hell" as well as the German words *Hoelle* (hell), *Hoeble* (cave), and *Holle* (the earth mother) are synonyms, which speak of the goddess of old.[15]

Marija Gimbutas has researched European prehistoric art and deciphered the meaning of decorative motifs used by artists on pottery, figurines, and cult objects since Paleolithic times. She refers to these motifs as the language of the Goddess. I love her book because it has given me insight into the inner world of my pre-Christian ancestors who lived so close to the earth and their visions, and who celebrated the underlying unity of all lifeforms in their worship of the Goddess. How sad that with the Christianization of Europe by the missionaries during the Roman occupation 2000 years ago, the Goddess was exiled and the intense love of this world for which she stood was declared unimportant in favor of the afterlife. The Goddess was banished from consciousness just like the Germanic god of ecstasy, Wodan, who was made into the Devil.[16] She

> gradually retreated into the depths of forests or onto mountain tops, where she remains to this day in beliefs and fairy stories. Human alienation from the vital roots of earthly life ensued, the results of which are clear in our contemporary society. But the cycles never stop turning, and now we find the Goddess reemerging from the forests and mountains, bringing us hope for the future, returning us to our most ancient human roots.[17]

The little girl, of course, did not know anything about this background against which her dream occurred and how close she was to that mysterious Divine Motherly Presence in her own unconscious. But the transpersonal powers in the depths of her soul called her and sent her through the black tunnel into the "womb of the earth" as if she were a part of the timeless shamanic tradition.

I like to think that the child had accumulated enough experiences of the radiant Earth in her grandmother's garden to comprehend intuitively that the soil, out of which so much Divine Beauty wells up for us, is sacred and safe. And that it was this knowledge which in her dream gave her the strength to land upright on her feet in the realm of the Goddess and to use her wits in coming to terms with what awaited her there.

Because now that she has reached the cave in the bowels of the Earth, she must meet the creative principle of Nature in the shape of fire and reach an agreement with it.

Looking at the dream one clearly sees that the "devil" there is not the Christian Devil at all. He had no similarity to the pictures of him which had been shown to her in pious books and religious magazines. Also, she had surely never heard of Wodan, the god of her pagan ancestors, since nothing unchristian was ever permitted in the home. The devil of her dream is an awesome column of living fire, reaching from the floor of the cave to its ceiling. It is the Life Force hidden in matter, and she must look at it and come to terms with it. As she approaches in fear and trembling a miracle happens: she receives an answer more compassionate and more humane than anything she had encountered so far in her short life.

That superhuman power in the heart of the Earth accepts her as a matter of fact. From now on she will serve it. This will be a new life for her. Because from now on she belongs to the Earth forever and only to the Earth. The alchemical kitchen in the depth of her own being has become her home and working place. There she works diligently with the fire and masters it: she cares for it, feeds it, keeps it clean, cherishes it, and uses it well. Transforming the raw into the cooked, she prepares nourishment for the God.

Sometimes these days when I work in solitude, transforming the raw stuff of my life and dreams into pictures, cooking the images, so to speak, until they are done and ready to be served, my hands are all sooty from the charcoal. Looking at them I think back to that first dream of mine and know that I am doing my job the way I am meant to. In other words, I "follow my bliss"[18] as Joseph Campbell would say.

But as a child I suffered terribly under the literal interpretation of my dream images by my Catholic tradition, having no way to read the meaning of the symbols and to translate them for conscious understanding. Who could have guessed then that the "journey to hell"[19] symbolized the descent into one's own interior, namely the unconscious, and that the column of living fire, called for lack of better terminology "devil," was a dream image of the life-force or libido.[20]

I also did not know how to help myself to understand what had happened to me in the dream, when I learned to read at the age of eight and a half years. I was given a book called *Bible History* that I read and reread many times. I remained, of course, stuck in the Catholic concepts and it never occurred to me to connect the column of living fire, which I had seen and experienced in the dream, with the many images of God as Fire in the Bible. It did not ring a bell when I read about the Pillar of Fire that lit the way for the Israelites by night on their journey through the desert. I did not make a connection when I read about the dialogue with the Presence in the Burning Thornbush, or the fiery flames that descended on the apostles and the Blessed Mother at Pentecost. I also did not link my journey into Hell with the descent of Jesus Christ to the same place after he had been crucified, had died, and was buried. I don't know why I had the Aha-experience only so much later in life, because I recited the Apostolic Creed, which says so, every night together with my grandmother, mother, and little sister, as we knelt before the Sacred Heart of Jesus on the hard wooden floor and prayed the rosary. I never connected my dream experience with this great mystery of the faith.

Today, of course, things are different. Edward F. Edinger's slim volumes *The Bible and the Psyche* and *The Christian Archetype*[21] are two of my favorite books. The psychological approach to the religious stories which shaped the spiritual life of the child has saved them for me. It gives them a profound new meaning that nourishes my soul.

I did not have much reading material. Aside from the *Bible History,* I was given a Roman Catechism, a Life of the Saints, a religious magazine called *City of God,* another one called *The Boy Jesus,* and the *Almanac of Saint Michael.* My mother had taught me reading from a children's Missal. The first word I read on my own was 'amen.' The Catechism soon became a source of suffering for me because my mother forced me to memorize it from the first to the last word, that is, not only the teachings, but also the questions that led up to them. With rod in hand she daily examined my progress.

But one day in 1947 a wonderful thing came into my life. My mother had a cleaning job at the Russian Commandant's place. In the basement there she found an old and torn copy of *Grimms' Fairy Tales* and brought it home. The cover and many pages were missing. But there were enough stories left in the book to make a difference in my life. I gobbled them up and reread them so many times that soon I knew them all by heart. My most beloved story was "Frau Holle." Years later when I was in school and the complete book came into my hands, the story of *Schneewittchen* (Little Snow-White) became my all-time favorite.

"Frau Holle" is the story of an unloved and mistreated girl who in her sorrow and despair jumps into a deep well, loses consciousness, and wakes up in a realm deep inside of the Earth. There she journeys until she reaches the house of the Earth Mother, whose name is Frau Holle. Mother Holle, who at first frightens the girl, soon reveals her loving kindness. The girl becomes her maidservant. After some time of serving Frau Holle diligently, the child is rewarded for her good work with pure gold. This she takes home with her as she returns into the daylight world.

Oh, how I loved that story. I remember lying awake at night and going into the tale with the help of my imagination until I felt with my whole being that I *was* the girl who pulled the freshly baked breads out of the oven, who shook the tree till the ripe red apples fell like rain, and who with both hands aired and shook Frau Holle's feather comforter at her window so vigorously that the feathers flew about and turned into snowflakes. I was in love with the season of winter and would sometimes sneak out of the house into the yard to watch the snow fall and feel it melt on my face and hands, all the while thinking, that *she* was right now shaking a big feather pillow out of her window to let the snowy stars drift over me, showering me with caresses, swaddling me in beauty.

By that time my childhood dream was forgotten. I did not even remember it when I read other fairy tales that told of adventures in Hell, of outwitting the Devil, and of journeys into the belly of the earth in search of gold, light, and other treasures. Three stories which I was fond of were "The Devil with the Three Golden Hairs," "The Blue Light," and "Snow-White and Rose-Red."[22] Though I loved these stories with a passion, it took me thirty years until I recognized the similarities between them and my dreams and realized how much they had helped me live.

I did not have a clue until one day one of my analysts upon hearing my dream exclaimed: "But it is just like the story of Frau Holle." And so it was. Upon seeing my dream amplified into a wider context, suddenly something "clicked" and everything fell into place. That was a life-giving experience for me because now I could feel my way with the dreams even though I did not yet have enough knowledge to understand them on my own. Another ten years would have to pass until I could grasp intellectually that my childhood dream portrayed the pattern of my life in shorthand: it was a gift of the Transpersonal Psyche, the Self, in anticipation of the future.

Struggling to understand that first dream of mine I had to learn the language of the soul which consists of symbols and metaphors. I found much in C. G. Jung's collected works that helped me towards an understanding of it as a shamanic journey; for example, the descent into the inward depth of the human soul was portrayed in it as a fall through a dark tunnel into Hell. I still remember the moment when it dawned on me that the devil of that dream was neither a person nor a metaphysical entity, but a numinous symbol of that part of the life force, which my Catholic tradition had rejected and suppressed, and in which C. G. Jung saw the dark and hidden side of God,[23] the missing Fourth of the Quaternity, and the Principle of Individuation. Edward Edinger's little book *The Creation of Consciousness*[24] offers a summary and profound interpretation of this subject matter and has become a friend to me.

When finally one day I read in the book *C. G. Jung Speaking* that Jung recommended that one establish "a healthy relationship with the devil,"[25] I had done enough inner work to comprehend the difficult terminology and grasp in a flash of sudden understanding that my first childhood dream had said this very same thing to me. Now I knew why that dream came to me over and over again for years: it prefigured a conscious relationship with the Transpersonal Psyche, initiating me into my very own inner depths, into the Mysteries of the Earth, and thus into the unfathomable resources of the unconscious, the soul.

Because I am a homemaker living an isolated life in a working class environment, I have to rely on books for intellectual stimulation and to support me in my search. I have drawn much comfort and strength from the writings of C. G. Jung when I could turn nowhere else for help. For instance, when I mourned the loss of my faith and was inconsolable, I came across the following sentences:

> I am not . . . addressing myself to the happy possessors of faith, but to those many people for whom the light has gone out, the mystery has faded, and God is dead. For most of them there is no going back, and one does not know either whether going back is the better way. To gain an understanding of religious matters, probably all that is left us today is the psychological approach. That is why I take these thought-forms that have become historically fixed, try to melt them down again and pour them into moulds of immediate experience.[26]

Next to Jung, it has been the work of Edward Edinger that has helped me most in understanding myself. He defines individuation simply as the "conscious dialectic relationship between ego and Self",[27] that is, "a mutual knowing between the ego and the Self."[28] Edinger's writings have become my companions. They have helped me to put my dreams into perspective, encouraged me to experience the reality of the objective psyche, justified my need to abandon myself to the flow of the life force, and supported me in my devotion to individuation as a way of life.[29] I have learned from him that strangely enough and contrary to popular opinion, the loss of one's faith and the inner emptiness that follows in its wake can be the road to a direct experience of the numinosum and an in-depth understanding of the Christian legacy. As Simone Weil put it: "In what concerns divine things, belief is not fitting. Only certainty will do. Anything less than certainty is unworthy of God."[30] Edinger's depiction of the human tortures that accompany the transformation process in the Transpersonal Psyche has reconciled me to the tragedies of my childhood and the miseries of my adult life.[31] I accept them because they have a meaning that calms a deep longing in my soul and wipes away my tears.

Looking at the dreams of my adult life, I can trace the elements of my childhood dream and their transformation in many of them. At this date my journals contain over two thousand dreams. I have chosen a small number of them for this book to give the reader some insight into the force that drives me to make the pictures. But they really offer only a brief glance at the pattern of my life, since the impression which the reader gets from those dreams is, of course, incomplete.

And that is as it has to be. Anyone can make his or her own experiment and undertake the inward journey to discover his or her own individual pattern in the unconscious. And this would really be much better than looking at someone else's. Inner work is a great adventure and well worth the time and effort it takes because it adds the elements of breathtaking mystery and wonder to daily life. In other words—it provides the fire. After a while it gives one a definite feeling for the infinite, that "inner guiding factor that is different from the conscious personality"[32] and which is the best ally and friend a person can have in life and in death.

To find this out has been a saving grace. Because no matter how well or not so well our life goes, no matter how lonely we are or how many friends we have or how many groups we belong to, ultimately each one of us is alone with his or her fate, the sorrows, the sufferings, and then death. We are all in need of a safe inner place and long to be consoled again and again. We have a desperate need to find out what it is that supports us when we can no longer support ourselves.[33]

Natural life grows in circles like a spiral. And so each time I paint a picture of the Black Madonna, the theme of my first childhood dream continues to expand: I am always taking another step inward, always delighting in what is found, always trying to see more of what is there, finding out how to live with it, and how to do it justice. I am insatiably curious about the psyche.

When I was a small girl in my grandmother's house I once sat before the only mirror she had. It was a free standing, full length mirror and I just loved it. Grandmother and Mother saw me looking at myself. They removed the mirror into the attic for good. They said that they were preventing me from falling into the sin of vanity. "Vanity of vanities, and all is vanity," my grandmother used to moan. And all the women in the family agreed, because they did not have any mirrors in the cloister either. I was taught to dress myself, to comb and braid my hair, and to keep myself neat as if blind.

Today, out of a basic need for truth and an immense longing for clarity, I create in my drawings and paintings mirrors of the soul. These soul mirrors get bigger all the time. I can't seem to make enough of them to finally see what is there.

In Grandmother's house there also hung that dreaded rod made from bare cut-off birch branches over the door. During the long years of my stay with her, the appearance of those dried up branches never changed, although the rod was replaced whenever it wore out. The rod was dead. But the bare bushes in the garden were alive. All winter long I watched their tiny buds to see them swell up in spring and burst into blossoms and leaves. Then they transformed themselves into little hard green berries, which tasted sour and took forever to change color and ripen. In the end though they always filled my hands with sweet fruit that sustained my heart, mind, and soul even more than my body.

I thought of that today, when I went up into the small room where I make my pictures. I had just gotten through scrubbing the kitchen floor and sat down to rest. As I looked around, my eyes fell on the bundles of ripe wheat and oats that hang on the walls. I had bought them three years ago at an outdoor farmers' market because I had fallen in love with their soft golden color. The old farmer said to me: "They make nice decorations and last forever. When they get dusty, just take them outside and let the wind blow through them. It will take the dust off and they will be as good as new." And so, when I came home that day from my shopping trip, I tied wheat, oats, sage, and babies' breath together with pieces of string into five bundles. I hung one high up on each wall to correlate with the four directions. And a fifth bundle I put into the tree-green vase that my husband made for me when our son was born and placed it on the table in the middle of the room. It pleased me to be surrounded by the wheat and oats. They had come fresh from the field; their seeds contained life itself; they smelled of the earth. I felt content, as if I were standing in a barn at harvest time or in my kitchen baking bread.

As I was looking up at these bundles of grain, I suddenly became aware that one of them is placed directly over the door of a walk-in closet. A thought went like electricity through my whole body, making me gasp with recognition: "But that is the rod from my childhood days! Look at that! Who would have guessed it! That barren instrument of torture has changed into this golden bundle, dappled by shade and sunlight filtering into the room through the tree outside the window. Just look at it! The curse has changed into a blessing. What a sacred thing I have in my house: it is life, eternal life!"

I could not help but smile: I had come home. I was where I wanted to be.

Aha! So that's how the unconscious works to weave all kinds of things together into the meandering pattern of one's destiny. What a pleasure to witness this process in one's own life. Three years ago I was not aware of any synchronicity. I was not at all conscious of what went on in my soul. I had simply done what came naturally, what felt right at the moment and gave me joy. But today I could see the child in me being amazed and delighted and I could see the rod transformed into pure living gold.

And that is how it goes. My childhood dream, the great dreams of my adult life, astounding synchronicities, and much inner work have taught me to trust in the movements of the life force in my own inner depth and to flow with that mystery. This state of being is the good and safe place, which that first dream promised me. I am content with that. It is much more than I ever dared to hope for. It just so happened that my life's journey has become the goal.

I do not claim to know any ultimate truth. And I like it that life is open-ended and that I do not know how things will turn out.

The journey goes on. New dreams are coming in the night and I am making new pictures.

Spring 1993

CHAPTER 16

My Personal Shield

My life is the story of the self-realization of the unconscious. Everything in the unconscious seeks outward manifestation, and the personality too desires to evolve out of its unconscious conditions and to experience itself as a whole.

C. J. JUNG,
Memories, Dreams, Reflections[1]

Planning the Shield

These introductory sentences to C.G. Jung's autobiography have moved me deeply ever since I first read them. Over the years I have sometimes repeated them to myself to justify my own involvement in soul-making. Like everyone else in our modern society, I am affected by the unspoken but ever-present commandment not to think about myself too much and especially not to spend time on something considered so vague and unknown as the psyche.

Therefore it often takes a great deal of courage on my part to tell my family and friends that I need to be alone, to leave the phone off the hook, shut off the doorbell, and maybe even cancel plans that I have already made. How else would it be possible for me to retreat into solitude when dreams and intuitions demand attention from me and urge me to make new pictures?

The time and energy it takes to do inner work cannot be given to other tasks which would be appreciated and rewarded by society. And so over the years I have mostly felt more burdened than blessed by the need of my soul and the inner obligation to make the individuation process visible in pictures.

But what can I do about it?

Today, like so often, I have retreated again into that tiny spare bedroom of our flat, which serves as my studio, to work on a new project: my personal shield.

It has been some time now since I decided to paint my personal myth in the shape of a shield. I have seen old Native American shields in the collection of our local museum as well as contemporary shields at powwows. And I like them. These wonderful creations grew out of vision quests.

People go into the wilderness to be alone and experience their inner essence in sacred dreams and visions. Like Jacob setting up a stone as a monument after his great dream of the ladder, they then paint shields. And since the North American soil is my chosen home, and I have come to understand my life as a constant vision quest, I find it appropriate to condense my personal myth into a shield for myself. When it is done, it will, of course, hardly resemble a Native American shield, because my unconscious is European.

Over the last couple of years I have made preparations for the shield. I once saw a tanned pigskin in a store. It was so soft to the touch and looked so lovely, that I simply had to have it. Then, when a large quilting hoop came into my hands, I stretched the pigskin over it. For months now it has been hanging on the wall of my room, patiently waiting to be painted.

Today I am ready.

The question is now: What dream images will best express my personal myth? Which ones shall I choose?

The Black Madonna will of course have to go in the center of my shield. But I would like to paint her as the Black Bear that has come to me in so many dreams lately. As I close my eyes to visualize her, the bear changes and becomes all golden.

This brings me to a special dream, in which I saw a new face of the Black Madonna that I had not known before. The dream did not occur spontaneously this time but was the result of dream incubation. I remember the circumstances which led up to it.

During the preceding day my mind had dwelt on some sorrows of my current life. I had been deeply disappointed by people whom I had considered my friends. They had put greed and their own advantage before human decency and integrity. This experience had shocked me; I had not expected it, and it hurt. From deep within me my old despair raised its voice: "And who watches over me?"

For some time now I have gotten into the habit of incubating dreams whenever I cannot solve a problem rationally or am put into a helpless position. What I do then is simply look at the issue which occupies me from all angles. In the evening I take time to come home to myself and write my thoughts in my journal. Then I formulate a short question and make a note of it so that I will still remember it the next morning. Knowing by now that dreams do not occur in a vacuum but are linked to all facets of my life, I concentrate intensely on the incubation phrase.

Blocking out all other thoughts and feelings, I repeat it over and over again like a mantra until I go to sleep. Should I wake up during the night before a dream has come, I again repeat the incubation phrase single-mindedly until I fall asleep. That is all.

On this particular evening I decided to use the spontaneous cry of my heart, "Who watches over me?" as the incubation phrase. What I dreamt, I had not expected:

> I dreamt I was in a house with some dear old friends of mine, when suddenly a big black bear walked in through the door. Everyone except me was scared to death; they all ran away to a safe place. I too was frightened but began to remember dreams of mine about the bear. I told myself that there was no reason to be afraid, since the bear is my power animal. I reminded myself to hold still and that this was a chance to make contact with a real live bear. So I let the bear come up to me and sniff me.
>
> Slowly I reached out with my right hand and touched her. Then I touched her again gently. The bear held still and let me do it. She came closer and closer to me and then snuggled up to me. I put my arms around her neck and hugged her. The bear pushed her big warm furry body against mine and hugged me back.
>
> While holding on to each other we then played together like children. We rolled over each other on the floor and tumbled on the rug joyfully. As I was holding on to the bear tighter and tighter, she looked me full in the eyes and very gently lay down on top of me, so that I had to bear her full weight. What immense power, and at the same time what loving kindness and gentleness!
>
> We hugged and hugged in the knowledge that we belonged together forever. Through my hands and body I got a thorough feeling for the size of her, for her roundness and softness, for her sweetness and playfulness and for her inexhaustible strength.
>
> Now the bear rose up and squatted on her enormous hind legs, raising her hands in blessing. I kept on hugging her. But she had grown so big in the meantime that I had to bend over backwards to see her face.
>
> And that was the moment when I discovered that her face had become human. It was completely round like the full moon, with a pale golden skin. That skin was extraordinarily fine, clear, and silky. Her eyes sat slightly slanted over lovely high cheekbones. The lips were full and softly rounded and lotus-flower pink. Her features were just so refined, positively elegant, and simultaneously exuded a touching innocence. Such grace!
>
> When I saw the sublime beauty of the face, I threw myself into her arms even deeper if possible. And we held on to each other and hugged to our hearts' content.
>
> Waking up, I realized immediately that I had looked into the Divine Face of the Kwan Yin.

I had this dream on September 3, 1990. And as I am planning my shield now, I know it must be this particular image of the Goddess as the great power that watches over me, which will go into the center of the shield.

But the blue ship which once came to me in a dream to tell me that I must do inner work also belongs in the center (Dream No. 7). I will have to paint myself standing before the Goddess and singing her praises (Dream No. 40), wearing the many-colored robe of her priestesses and priests (Dream No. 46).

I must add my shaman's drum (Dream No. 48) and make it simultaneously into a large round mirror in my right hand. Because this is how I serve her: I hold a mirror up to her in my pictures so that she can contemplate her face. And of course I must not forget the three-and-a-half-year-old little girl who dreamt my first childhood dream and who is forever with me. I will put cherry blossoms in her little fists and paint her redeemed and dancing in the middle of my heart.

The beater will be a branch carrying two ripe yellow pears, symbols for the harvest which has finally arrived after so much inner work and waiting. These pears have appeared in several dreams.

I can visualize the central image of my shield clearly now and see that in order to express my name *Tataya Mato* (Dream No. 38) fully, I must add the breath flowing in a gentle stream from the face of the Goddess with myself in it. She breathes me out; she sings me. And I am struck by this vivid metaphor for the self-realization of the unconscious.

As I continue to imagine how the central image will look, I know that it will have to sit on a night black background, symbol of the unconscious and the Earth. I want to surround it with a big rainbow and four open roses filled with honey for the people (Dream No. 12). The roses will hold clear rock crystals in their centers.

The last thing I would need to do to complete the shield in an authentic manner would be to decorate the rim with feathers or bear claws as I have seen on shields in the museum and at powwows. But I am not an Indian and so I cannot do that. I must round out the process and put on the finishing touches by drawing on my own inner resources.

In my sewing basket I have hidden a treasured remnant of cotton of a kind which I cannot find in fabric stores any more. I love it so much. It is woven in rainbow colors but they are muted so masterfully that they resemble earth tones. I will sew three ribbons from it and add them like prayer flags to the rim. They will always remind me of my name when they flutter in the wind in personal rituals.

And so I know now how the shield will look. I have already sewn the ribbons. What is left to do is to get the tubes of acrylic paint out of the drawer and some brushes from the vase in which I store them and go to work.

Last year, my editor and dear friend, Louise Mahdi, made me the gift of a wonderful book, *The Language of the Goddess,* by Marija Gimbutas. This book helped me to amplify my dreams further than I had been able to do before and to understand them in the timeless context of human inner experience. It describes the many faces of the Goddess as people have experienced and envisioned her through the millennia in ancient times. In it I found a chapter on the bear as the primeval Mother.[2]

I also came across some other information that is helpful to me in understanding my dreams. In the first of his thirteen final lectures in *Transformations of Myths through Time,* Joseph Campbell talks about the prehistoric cave chapels dedicated to the bear in the high Alps of Silesia.[3] I had not known about them and now wonder if some of my distant ancestors may have worshipped there, because I have roots in Upper Silesia as well as in Russia.

I have had dreams lately in which shaman ancestors of mine are coming from as far away as Siberia to America, seeking and finding me. They demand from me that I continue their tradition. They go to great lengths in the dreams to transmit their power to me, to bring me their ceremonial objects for future use, even to teach me how to drum and heal. They insist that I am part of that great unbroken chain of shamans reaching back into prehistoric times, those times which Marija Gimbutas has researched.

What is going on here? Are dreams like this to be taken literally or symbolically? I do not know. But I know one thing, namely, that I have to hold on to the light of clear thinking vis-à-vis the unconscious. At this point in my life I really do not know what to do with such dreams, except of course to draw or paint them, because that will in time lead to a more complete understanding of the psyche on my part.

Today I am not worrying about that. I am just so glad to finally be able to paint my shield. On the back of it I shall write two sentences which I love so much that I repeat them often to myself.

The first one is a phrase written by the German poet Rainer Maria Rilke: *"Wie dunkeln und rauschen im Instrument die Waelder seines Holzes."*[4] This means, loosely translated, "Oh, how the forests darken and murmur in the wood of the musical instrument."

The second one is a line from the motet "Jesu meine Freude" by Johann Sebastian Bach: *"Tobe Welt und springe, ich steh hier und singe."*[5] And this means "Go on and rage like mad, world. Here I stand and sing my song."

Contemplating the Finished Shield

The images which I painted on my shield came from several dreams. I have just described how I first planned and visualized it. What I could not foresee at that time was how my hands would give shape to my personal myth. As I look now at the finished shield, I am surprised and delighted at how it turned out.

163

163. *My Personal Shield* (Acrylic on pigskin, July 23, 1991)

The Great Bear has the pale golden face of the Kwan Yin as I saw Her in a dream. Her body shines in many shades of gold. They remind me of the moon, ripe wheat and oat stalks, clover honey, white currants, basswood blossoms, wine, pear liqueur, beeswax candles, corn silk, sunflower oil, the flesh of ripe plums, sugar maples in fall, and bushelbaskets full of grain at harvest time. She seems to be made from a soft golden light that has come out of the night-black background.

From Her face flows clear breath which passes through the royal blue ship of transcendence. The breath becomes the woman Tataya Mato, whose name means 'Bear Wind' or 'Breath of the Bear' or 'Rainbow.' And so Tataya wears the golden-hued robe of many colors and holds her shaman's drum, which is a clear mirror, in her right hand. She beats the drum gently for the Black Madonna with her pears.

To me Tataya looks almost like a ripe pear too, food for the Goddess. Brought forth by Her, she will be absorbed back into the Mother when her life's work is done and the time is ripe. Tataya carries in her heart the little girl of three and a half years, who long ago suffered so much, and who is now as clear and fine as transparent rock crystal, as the mirror, and as the breath of the Bear. The child dances with joyful abandon, holding a branch from her cherry tree loaded with white golden-hued blossoms. The white roses around the Great Bear are all golden-hued too and brimming with honey. Even the rainbow looks to me as if it were woven of pure light filtering through the golden leaves of a sugar maple on a warm and clear autumn day.

I have hung the shield on a white wall. At dusk it becomes even more luminous. When the room is almost completely dark, one can still see the Bear and Her rainbow of roses faintly glow. And there seems to be a halo around the shield.

Summer 1991

CHAPTER 17

Excerpts from My Dream Journals

To concern ourselves with dreams is a way of reflecting on ourselves—a way of self-reflection. It is not our ego-consciousness reflecting on itself; rather, it turns its attention to the objective actuality of the dream as a communication or message from the unconscious, unitary soul of humanity. It reflects not on the ego but on the self; it recollects that strange self, alien to the ego, which was ours from the beginning, the trunk from which the ego grew. It is alien to us because we have estranged ourselves from it through the aberrations of the conscious mind.

—C. G. JUNG[1]

The following ninety-two dreams and active imaginations recorded over a twenty-year period from 1973 to 1993, are among those which are always with me. They have shaped my life to such an extent that I live with them and they live with me. All of these and many others that are recorded in my dream journals have inspired my pictures. To give an overview, I am first listing the dreams by title. The full descriptions then follow.

List of Dreams by Title

1. *THE GOLDEN-GREEN PLANT STONE WEEPS (7-27-1973)*

2. *THE CÕQUECOI: I HAVE TO SEARCH FOR SUN AND MOON IN THE CATHEDRAL ON THE MOUNTAIN (10-14-1973)*

3. *OCEAN WAVES AS HIGH AS THE ALPS (12-27-1973)*

4. *THE OCEAN GIVES ME THREE BLACK RINGS (2-3-1974)*

5. *THE EARTH CATHEDRAL (3-15-1974)*

6. *THE BLACK AND THE WHITE CHRIST EMBRACE ON THE CROSS (6-11-1974)*

7. *THE BLUE SHIP ASKS ME TO DO INNER WORK (1-13-1977)*

8. *MY MASTERS: LIGHTNING AND THUNDER (7-30-1977)*

9. *THE SANCTUARY OF THE DARK MOTHER OFFERS SAFETY AND REDEMPTION (8-2-1979)*

10. *THE BLUE-VIOLET FIRE FROM BELOW (11-7-1979)*

11. *A MASS IN HONOR OF SOPHIA (11-30-1979)*

12. *I HAVE INHERITED CAULDRONS TO MAKE HONEY (12-8-1979)*

13. *THE RED-HUED RAINBOW BIRD FROM ABOVE (1-1-1980)*

14. *WODAN GUIDES ME THROUGH THE TREE (2-2-1980)*

15. *THE WELL OF PICTURES IS THE EYE OF THE EARTH (2-8-1980)*

16. *THE BLACK BUFFALO CARRIES ME OUT OF THE CHURCH (5-3-1980)*

17. *I AM MARKED AS A SIGN THAT I BELONG TO WODAN (5-16-1980)*

18. *THE GIANT BIRD IN THE ANCIENT TREE (9-3-1980)*

19. *THE EARTH SPLITS OPEN IN THE SHAPE OF A CROSS (9-10-1980)*

20. *I HAVE TO PAINT THE SUFFERING BLACK GODDESS FOR THE WHITE CHURCH (3-21-1981)*

21. *ACTIVE IMAGINATION: THE MASS OF THE BLACK MADONNA (3-27-1981)*

22. *ACTIVE IMAGINATION: THE SUFFERING BLACK MADONNA UNDERNEATH CHICAGO (3-28-1981)*

23. *PICTURES FOR THE REDEMPTION OF THE GODDESS (3-29-1981)*

24. *I HAVE TO EAT THE BLACK MADONNA (4-4-1981)*

25. *THE BLACK MADONNA ON TRIAL (5-11-1981)*

26. *THE EARTH CATHEDRAL IS BEING RESTORED (5-25-1981)*

27. *THE SACRED CAVE OF THE BROTHERHOOD (6-13-1981)*

28. *THE FUSION OF BREAD AND WINE BY A SHAFT OF LIGHT (6-23-1981)*

29. *ACTIVE IMAGINATION: THE BIG BLACK MOTHER WITH LOVERS IN HER HAIR (7-21-1981)*

30. *THE BLACK MADONNA LOOKS AT ME (8-13-1981)*

31. *THE HANDS OF THE BLACK MADONNA, THE CREATOR (8-31-1981)*

32. *THE SIXTEEN DISGUISES OF THE BLACK MADONNA (9-19-1981)*

33. *I SEW LITURGICAL VESTMENTS FOR THE PRIESTESSES OF THE BLACK MADONNA (10-1-1981)*

34. *THE CRYSTAL WITH THE FIERY HEART INSIDE (5-7-1982)*

35. *THE EARTH CATHEDRAL IS FINISHED (4-29-1982)*

36. *THE CONJUNCTIO (7-1-1983)*

37. *ACTIVE IMAGINATION: THE BLACK MADONNA SPEAKS TO ME ABOUT MY MOTHER (3-18-1984)*

38. *I AM GIVEN A NEW NAME: TA DAYA WADO (11-16-1984)*

39. *I FIGHT FOR THE ASSUMPTION OF MARY (11-18-1984)*

40. *SINGING THE PRAISES OF THE BLACK MADONNA (11-25-1984)*

41. *A TREE GROWS OUT OF A BLACK POOL IN THE CHURCH (12-25-1984)*

42. *MY VERY OWN HOLY BOOK (2-19-1988)*

43. *I AM A SHAMAN OF THE BLACK MADONNA (5-1-1988)*

44. *ACTIVE IMAGINATION: THE BLACK MADONNA ASCENDS FROM UNDERNEATH CHICAGO AND IS FREE (8-27-1988)*

45. *ACTIVE IMAGINATION: THE GOLDEN TIPI OF RECONCILIATION (8-27-1988)*

46. *I AM A PRIESTESS OF THE BLACK MADONNA (12-29-1988)*

47. *ACTIVE IMAGINATION: THE BLACK MADONNA, WHITE BUFFALO WOMAN, THE KWAN YIN, AND THE SHEKINAH HAVE COME TO HEAL THE EARTH (4-13-1989)*

48. *THE BLACK MADONNA'S DRUM AND MY DRUM ARE CONNECTED (4-26-1989)*

49. *THE BLACK MADONNA HEALS ME AND MANY OTHER PEOPLE WITH HER VEIL (5-4-1989)*

50. *THE CHRIST CHILD, WHICH IS THE BLACK MADONNA AS A LITTLE GIRL (9-28-1989)*

Full Descriptions of the Dreams

1. *THE GOLDEN-GREEN PLANT STONE WEEPS (7-27-1973)*

   I dreamt that together with my husband and our little son I had to return to Germany for at least a year. We packed the suitcases and went to say good-bye to our friends. On the way there I had to work hard not to fall down a slope, because I was forced to retrieve my coaster wagon which jumped all by itself downhill from one serpentine curve to another. After we had taken leave of our friends, we walked back on a blacktopped street up a hill.

   On top of that hill we saw crystals growing out of the street surface. They covered an area of about one square yard. We had noticed them before on the way downhill, but had not stopped or paid attention to them.

   The crystals were golden-green, clear, and transparent. All that traffic going over them had split, broken, and flattened them into the asphalt.

   I bent down to pick one up, but could not do it. An unseen presence interfered, saying that they were poisonous or dangerous and should not be touched. Clear tears trickled out of the crystals.

   Suddenly a person unknown to me stood next to me and my husband. That person began to dig the crystals up, but got at them from underneath. I had always tried to touch them from above, and each time was forced to withdraw my hand when the warning came. This unknown person succeeded in lifting one of the bigger stones, which was the size of three or four fists, out of the ground. The crystal was not broken at all, but absolutely whole and perfect. It shone with an inner light. It had roots like seaweed. They grew as a thick bundle out of the bottom of the rock. The invisible presence said: "These stones have roots and they are still growing."

   I then suddenly became conscious that I had discovered in my research the one link in the evolution from rock to plant which still had been missing. Here was a plant-stone or stone-plant. It was now safe for me to carry that precious stone in my hands, as long as I did not touch it from above.

With great reverence I contemplated the mysterious living crystal in my hands and was filled with pure joy.

2. THE CŌQUECOI: I HAVE TO SEARCH FOR SUN AND MOON IN THE CATHEDRAL ON THE MOUNTAIN (10-14-1973)

I dreamt that I met an unknown man on a street halfway up a mountain. He rode a bicycle, had come from the left, and was going uphill. I was dressed in work clothes and work shoes and was on my way downhill.

Upon reaching a low building at the foot of the mountain, I saw an open black briefcase on the ground leaning against the wall. A postcard stuck out of one of its compartments. I bent down and read it. It was a message written to me by that unknown man whom I had just met. He had already reached his destination, which was the Cathedral on the Mountain where the Cōquecoi was being worshipped.

That low building at the foot of the mountain was built into the earth and only its roof and an entrance were visible. I opened the door and entered. It was dark inside. But in the wall to my left I saw a very beautiful Gothic church window. It was divided into four squares by a cross. Each square was a picture made of stained glass. I only remember the upper right one. There sun and moon were in the process of coming together into a unity, and this process was breaking down a tower. It tumbled down. A mysterious light coming from an unknown source within the earth made the window glow. Sun and moon shone in wonderful golden yellows and oranges. They had mysterious black signs painted right into them.

An invisible presence said: "This is the Cōquecoi. It is powerful and victorious. It lives in the Cathedral on the Mountain. You have to search for it."

I asked my husband to accompany me on my quest for the Cōquecoi, but he did not want to.

(It took me ten years to find out the meaning of the strange word "Cōquecoi". The solution was given through dream No. 36 on 7-1-1983).

3. OCEAN WAVES AS HIGH AS THE ALPS (12-27-1973)

I dreamt that I went to the ocean on a lovely clear summer day to take a swim. But upon reaching the beach, I decided I had better forget about it because the sea turned out to be a boiling infinity.

Suddenly an unknown man stood next to me and together we watched the waters. The ocean was terrible but also wonderful to behold. Giant waves rose from inside of it, as if they were huge springs welling up out of the deepest depths. It was an unearthly boiling. The waves shot straight up like mountains and as high as the Alps. Then they would fall back into unfathomable depths again.

This took place everywhere: on the horizon as well as close by, in the middle of the sea as well as near the shore. But to our right we saw a city built on firm land.

There was no wind at all. Nothing moved or touched the waters from outside. Those uncanny movements rose entirely out of the innermost depths of the ocean.

It was self-evident that any attempt on my part to swim or take a boat ride would end in death.

Suddenly we saw a woman swimming at the edge of the sea. She wore a life preserver like a big ring around her waist. That shiny round shape floated safely on the water and supported her in its center. The woman was totally relaxed. With her arms wide open she simply let herself be carried by the currents. My companion and I talked about this, as the woman drifted from the far right to the far left, then back and forth again.

But after a while she seemed to disappear under one of those giant waves. I could still see the edge of her life preserver shine through the water and remain floating in the same spot.

To my great surprise I suddenly saw that what hid the woman from our view was not water at all, but a cloud of vapor. And now mountains of vapor began to rise everywhere on that wide sea. The infinity had become calm and had taken its movements back into its own depths. The ocean was now still and its surface barely rippled. Lovely white clouds rose everywhere on the vast expanse. And they drifted upward.

4. THE OCEAN GIVES ME THREE BLACK RINGS (2-3-1974)

I dreamt that I was taking a walk among the sand dunes of a beach on which the ocean had deposited beautiful stones. A big dune to my left had been half opened and I saw those wet stones glistening in the sand. I began to gather some of them up. They were rock crystals that had been polished by the water into smooth ovals. Each of them was half black and half clear. Their transparent beauty filled me with great joy. Suddenly I found three rings among them which had been cut out of rock crystal. They belonged together, were deep black on the outside, but totally clear and transparent inside. I put them on my left ring finger and wore them together with my gold wedding band.

I also discovered a set of three magnifying lenses that were perfect squares. They had been carefully cut out of a single large rock crystal and then polished to perfection. They were of different thicknesses and powers. The lenses were absolutely clear and the rims black.

I loved these gifts of the ocean and took them with me.

5. THE EARTH CATHEDRAL (3-15-1974)

I dreamt that I stood before an ancient Cathedral of extraordinary beauty. It was much, much older than even the oldest Romanesque cathedrals of Europe. My husband and little son were with me. What we could see from the outside seemed to be only the uppermost part with the roof because most of the huge Cathedral was hidden in the earth. The part above ground had been painted in earth colors. Thick columns ran up to the roof. We walked along those colorful walls and columns and could not get enough of looking at them. I touched the walls with both hands and held on to them because I was so moved. I did not want to leave.

That Cathedral stood on a hill. A little lower was an ancient wall from which one could see the city. That low moss-covered wall was the meditation place of an old hermit who liked to contemplate the clear quartz crystals growing out of its top surface. They were all perfect cubes of different sizes. Always two of them grew together: a big one and a little one. I walked to the wall alone and contemplated the crystals in silence. My husband and son did not pay any attention to them.

Ahead of us we saw an ancient bridge that led over a shallow river into the city. Before we crossed it, I turned around to look once more at the Earth Cathedral. A voice said: "This Cathedral grew all by itself like a primeval forest."

6. THE BLACK AND THE WHITE CHRIST EMBRACE ON THE CROSS (6-11-1974)

I dreamt that I walked into the Romanesque cathedral of Limburg/Lahn in Germany. Its inside walls were covered with beautifully painted ancient pictures. They were unfamiliar to me. On my left I saw a huge cross with Jesus Christ on it. His skin was black.

I also dreamt of another big cross. But instead of one, there were two Christs hanging on it. They were alive. One of them was white, the other black. To my great astonishment they embraced and kissed each other.

7. THE BLUE SHIP ASKS ME TO DO INNER WORK (1-13-1977)

I dreamt that I was standing on the shore of the ocean. An ancient blue ship with innumerable royal blue sails came swimming across the waters to me. This ship was a living, beating heart. I saw it pulsating. It had come from far away to talk to me. It said, it was my true essence. With great urgency it begged me to spend time on meditation. Its fate depended on my inner work and that was its only chance to reach its goal.

8. MY MASTERS: LIGHTNING AND THUNDER (7-30-1977)

I dreamt that I had gone on an outing into the woods with some friends from a fundamentalist Catholic movement. A storm began to brew. Fearing for our safety, we quickly got into our group leader's van and headed home. The car was moving fast when a flash of lightning came out of the dark clouds on the horizon. We saw that flash and heard the thunder. To my great amazement, lightning and thunder remained visible and took on solid shape, connecting the sky with the ground. They looked like slender columns which began literally to walk in our direction and soon caught up with the speeding van.

There were three columns. In the center was the lightning, a column of pure living fire, reaching from the earth into the dark thunder clouds. To the right and left of it were the thunders, two black columns of pure living darkness, also connecting earth and sky. It soon became clear that they were after me. And so my friends forced me to leave the van. They simply abandoned me and drove away as fast as they could. I was shaking with terror.

I had no choice but to kneel down before the overwhelming powers and to touch the column of fire with my forehead as a sign of my submission. As soon as I did that, I felt fiery energy stream into my whole body. And when the lightning and thunder began to walk away, I followed them.

They led me into solitude for two days and instructed me about my life. They told me that they were my masters and that it was my destiny to be a solitary. In the future I would wander all over the earth as a poor, independent monk and a relative to all beings. Then they gave me a simple brown, woolen handwoven and handsewn robe like the one St. Francis wore.

During the two days that I lived with my masters, fear changed into love. I accepted my fate and did everything they told me.

9. THE SANCTUARY OF THE DARK MOTHER OFFERS SAFETY AND REDEMPTION (8-2-1979)

I dreamt that a group of young thugs on motorcycles tormented me. I could have escaped them had I only entered the Chapel of the Dark Mother that stood next to the street. The path leading to that chapel was framed by trees bearing huge, ripe, red raspberries. In the Sanctuary people venerated the Dark Mother. She offered safety and redemption to anyone who fled to her.

10. THE BLUE-VIOLET FIRE FROM BELOW (11-7-1979)

I dreamt that I was on an outing together with some friends. We were visiting an ancient cathedral on a mountain and sitting at some tables close to a fireplace in the anteroom talking. When my friends left in their cars to go home, I stayed behind for a while, contemplating the fireplace in which a piece of wood standing upright in a circle of glowing embers burned peacefully. I then had to leave too, because it was getting dark outside. As I walked to my car I could still see the fire shining through a low window in one of the cathedral walls.

Suddenly I saw the fire spread. It grew huge and then I heard the sound of a tremendous explosion. In the middle of the red and gold leaping flames of the fireplace appeared a second fire with intense blue flames that were violet around the edges. This blue fire shot up out of the cathedral basement. The fire from the fireplace had eaten through the heavy stone floor and linked up with the electricity that ran through thick cables in the basement.

Suddenly an unknown young man was at my side. I had somehow entered the cathedral on my own and he had come to help me find my way. Together we went through many dark and narrow passageways and up and down stairways as if we were going through a labyrinth. He used a stick made of raw wood to pry trap doors open, so that we could move forward freely. We stuck closely together; we helped each other; we worked fast. It was very helpful that he knew all the twists and turns on our way through the dark and hidden parts of the cathedral. Finally we emerged outside again in broad daylight.

We walked once around the whole church in a circle so that we saw its backside too. Having arrived at the front again, we watched the fire raging inside of the cathedral, destroying everything. But the thick stone walls prevented the fire from spreading into the neighborhood. The people living close by had nothing to fear and continued to go about their daily business.

The fire had begun on the left side of the cathedral, then swept through the main part and had now reached the right side, where it was destroying the biggest and most beautiful of all the altars: the altar of the Holy Trinity and the Blessed Mother.

When I looked up, I saw a very old, white-haired woman looking out of one of the cathedral windows. She watched over the fire and allowed it to take its course. Her house was connected with that big church and was a secret part of it, although it belonged totally to her. She knew a hidden way from her dwelling place into the cathedral. She could go in and out of it whenever it pleased her.

11. A MASS IN HONOR OF SOPHIA (11-30-1979)

I did active imagination and returned to the ancient cathedral on the mountain. Its inside was completely burnt out—all the altars had been destroyed. It was now totally empty and the walls were blackened by soot. The ancient woman was there and told me we would have to wash and scrub the whole church clean for future use. She provided a pail of water and rags. So I went down on my knees and scrubbed the floor, while she washed the walls, columns, and ceiling. She did most of the work and never permitted me to climb a ladder. At one point I wondered what her name was. She turned around and said loud and clear: ''Sophia.'' When she had washed the old Romanesque windows too, bright light streamed freely into the large empty space of the cathedral. The windows glowed with an intense beauty and I saw that they showed Christian and pagan images unified into an organic whole.

In the center of the crossing lay a square slab of rock right underneath the highest of the seven towers. Sophia had put a pillow and a blanket on it for me.

When I had gotten this far in active imagination, I fell asleep. I dream that I am flying my own airplane and am just getting off the ground. I go up and on doing so look down. I see a group of gypsy women in long dresses as colorful as red-hued rainbows. They are waving to me. There is a little gypsy girl of about four and another one of about ten years of age. There are a gypsy teenager and a young woman. There is a middle-aged gypsy woman and an older one and then a real old one. But right in the middle of them all I see the oldest gypsy of them all, Sophia, her face so finely wrinkled and surrounded by a halo of white hair under her veil. They all smile at me and wave to me as they see me go up. They are my friends and are going to go hiking in the mountains. The next thing I know is that I have reached a place where a mass will be celebrated in honor of Sophia. The altar is a square slab of rock in the center of the room. Many people have gathered and are waiting for the mass to begin.

12. I HAVE INHERITED CAULDRONS TO MAKE HONEY (12-8-1979)

I dreamt that I discovered the place in the old country where the man whom I loved had died. He had been the maker of honey and used to cook it up in three or four cauldrons on the market square in the center of a small medieval town in Germany. I was his widow and filled with great grief. But when I entered his house, his essence and spirit were tangibly waiting for me. They came to me, embraced me, and comforted me.

I had inherited the house and the cauldrons from him and if I wanted to, I could start to cook up honey and go into production right away. It was all there waiting for me. It would not be at all difficult to go into business. The people who had worked for him knew all the details and were there to help me.

I was amazed at the foresight with which my late husband had prepared my inheritance. I was deeply moved by his love for me and his presence. I saw it hovering in the room, completely alive, and the reality of it made the tears run down my cheeks.

13. THE RED-HUED RAINBOW BIRD FROM ABOVE (1-1-1980)

I dreamt that I was crossing a big bridge over a valley together with an unknown man. This bridge was also a park. To our right many song birds flew through the air and landed on the railing of the bridge and in the trees. Suddenly there appeared a huge bird from behind us in the sky to our left. Her long feathers shone in all the colors of the rainbow but were at the same time red, so that she looked like a red-hued rainbow. She wore a crown of feathers on her head, and my companion told me that she belonged to the woodpecker family.

She had extraordinary and unusual abilities and longed to show us what she was capable of doing. She made eye contact with us and I liked the clear intelligence that shone from those eyes. She flew upside down towards the right, that is, with her back turned towards the Earth and her belly towards the sky. Her red plumage of many colors sparkled golden in the sun above the green grass of the park.

The bird then touched the ground for a split second with her back, and when she rose into the air again, still flying with her belly turned towards the sky, she threw her crown down for me. Then she turned over into the regular flying position of birds, rose higher and higher and flew away. When I picked up the crown and examined it, I saw that it was a mature one which she had shed like a ripe fruit. I was filled with great joy and took the crown home with me.

14. WODAN GUIDES ME THROUGH THE TREE (2-2-1980)

I dream I am inside a huge tree, going down deeper and deeper towards the roots. This is Wodan's realm and I know it. There are many rooms and chambers in the tree, connected by stairways and doors. All the doors are open to me, so I can go as deep down as I please. I descend, chanting the name of Wodan. The name is alive and vibrating inside of me like the sound of an ancient cathedral bell. This sound guides me. The rooms that I reach are filled with ancient knowledge and wisdom. I can trust this presence. I am safe. I am making the journey inside the tree with the help of Wodan, who walks at my side. He is a dark-skinned sage from the Himalayan mountains and has the compassionate eyes of Jesus Christ. He also wears the long white robe of Christ. He guides me with his greater knowledge and power. Therefore I can go where no one else can go.

15. THE WELL OF PICTURES IS THE EYE OF THE EARTH (2-8-1980)

I dreamt that the German expressionist painter Max Beckmann was working next to a well. This well reached into the unfathomable depths of the Earth and was simultaneously an eye. It was not circular but oval in shape. Its walls had been built from rust-red rocks. I looked into that well and saw the iris of the eye as a large bright circle. The pupil in its center consisted of the dark water. Max Beckmann stood to the right and looked with great concentration into the well. He saw pictures coming up out of the depths which he then painted. The well was the eye of the Earth, looking at us, the sky, and the universe. And it was alive.

16. THE BLACK BUFFALO CARRIES ME OUT OF THE CHURCH (2-3-1980)

I dreamt that my husband and I drove to a church on a warm and lovely summer day. He parked the car. While he was locking it, I walked towards the church. To our left stood a group of people chatting.

Suddenly a very powerful young black buffalo came charging from the left towards the people, sped past them and in our direction. His eyes and small horns were gleaming. He had a shiny coat of strong black hair and was full of unbelievable energy.

I ran towards the church for safety while looking back and calling out to my husband to get quickly into the car, which he did. I entered the church and tried to lock the heavy wooden doors behind me. But no matter how many times I tried to work the old iron lock into place, I could not do it. So I ran up another stairway and through a second door, also made of heavy wood. It too had an old strong iron lock. Again I did not succeed in locking the door for safety, no matter how often I tried. I had to run up more stairways and through a third door, which again I could not lock behind me. By now I was desperate. I feared the buffalo and had the gut feeling that he would come after me. Luckily I found an ancient heavy wooden club with metal spikes and grabbed it. At least now I had a weapon to defend myself against the animal if he really came after me. I saw another long flight of stairs, ran up those stone steps and through many more doors to reach a safe place, but again it was not in my power to lock a single door behind me for protection. Finally I had reached the highest place in the church and there was nowhere else to go. Suddenly I saw many other people in the church and breathed a sigh of relief. I felt that I could count on them to help me should I need them. I ended up in a tiny room with big old doors and a strong metal lock. Even this very last door I could not lock. But the presence of so many good Catholics calmed and reassured me.

Then I heard the buffalo enter the church and race up the stairs to get me. His hoofs were pounding on the stone steps like thunder. I heard him push through all those doors.

When the people realized that he was coming, they did something terrible to me. Looking out only for themselves, they abandoned me by taking my only defense away from me. They wrenched the wooden club out of my hands. When the buffalo came into the room I was in, I cried out to the people to have mercy and help me. But they were all stone-faced and no one moved. So the buffalo picked me up and laid me across his neck and carried me away. The people were all relieved that he did not touch them. He did not want them. He wanted just me and carried me down all those stairways and out of the church.

This young buffalo was not only full of fire but highly intelligent. His eyes shone with an inner light. He knew exactly what he was doing. He had come from far away to claim me and take me with him. I had no power to resist. Perhaps, after what I had been through, I did not even want to resist him.

17. *I AM MARKED AS A SIGN THAT I BELONG TO WODAN (5-16-1980)*

I dreamt that a big hand holding a knife came towards me and marked me from head to toe by cutting two deep parallel lines into my flesh. I was being marked as a sign that I belonged to Wodan. This meant that the natural flow of life would be within me.

18. *THE GIANT BIRD IN THE ANCIENT TREE (9-3-1980)*

I dreamt that my husband and I were journeying to an ancient woods near the ocean. We were searching for a certain tree. All we knew was that it existed, that we loved it, and that we simply had to find it.

There it was! From afar we could see the forest and that giant tree growing right in the center of it. The tree was of such an immense height that it touched the sky. It had grown for millions of years and connected Heaven and Earth. It stood in full bloom. Thousands of snowy blossoms shimmered between the green leaves in the sunlight. At the very top of the tree sat a huge white bird. She had the shape of a songbird, but who she was, we knew not. She moved among the leaves and hopped from branch to branch. My husband and I planned to pitch a tent in order to stay close to that tree for a while. It was raining a lot.

19. *THE EARTH SPLITS OPEN IN THE SHAPE OF A CROSS (9-10-1980)*

   I dreamt that I was kneeling on the ground and digging a hole with my bare hands. I knew that the pictures which I had to paint were hidden in the earth. This was the way to reach them. Suddenly the earth split open all by itself into the four directions from the hole in the center. It looked like an even-armed cross. The earth was doing that to help me reach the paintings more easily. I could even enter into the ground right there. And I did that. Deep inside of the earth I reached tunnels. They were paths through some kind of a maze. Except it was not a maze, but a treasure house. And all the pictures were stored right there on the walls of those tunnels. I could see well because a gentle light, coming from within the earth, was shining. The only thing I had to do was to take one picture at a time and carry it up and out into the daylight. That was my vocation, the work which I had to do in the future.

   I also dreamt that I was cooking all my life experiences in a big cauldron over an open fire. And I was stirring the pot.

20. *I HAVE TO PAINT THE SUFFERING BLACK GODDESS FOR THE WHITE CHURCH (3-21-1981)*

   I dreamt that my husband, my son, and I were trying out new cars. My husband had brought two along so we could find out which one would suit us best. There was a regular yellow car and a very special green jeep which was unusual in that it could be adjusted in many different ways to suit different situations. We decided that the jeep was just right for us and that we would buy it.

   We tried the cars out in a place called "Holy Hill." This was a hill or mountain on which a sanctuary of the Blessed Mother was built. The church was big and completely white. It was a holy place to which many pilgrims came to venerate the Blessed Mother. Priests and monks took care of it. My husband and son returned the yellow car and I was left with the jeep. I tried it out on the road by the great white church. I was scared at first when I tried to handle it, but it was all right.

   I then left the car and entered the sanctuary. When I got inside I suddenly understood that my paintings of the suffering Black Goddess were very important. I knew that this was the place for which I was to paint them. My pictures would be brought into this church and hung there for the pilgrims to see and contemplate.

   There was another church in a nearby city and I understood that I had to make pictures for that church too. These were also to be pictures of the Suffering Black Madonna. I had these pictures all in my mind and was carrying them around in my heart. I understood how important it was to paint them and to exhibit them in the churches for the people.

21. *ACTIVE IMAGINATION: THE MASS OF THE BLACK MADONNA (3-27-1981)*

   I see the Black Mother at a table, lighting two candles. The Holy Day has come. She puts them in the middle of the table where they shine in the darkness. She blesses the cup of wine laced with fire, and gives a drink to all her children who are waiting for her around the table. Then she feeds them the bread and feeds them with herself. This is the Mass.

22. *ACTIVE IMAGINATION: THE SUFFERING BLACK MADONNA UNDERNEATH CHICAGO (3-28-1981)*

   I am doing active imagination. Suddenly I see a megalopolis. It is Chicago. Underneath that giant city, deep inside the earth, I see a dark vault. Squeezed into that narrow dark vault is the Black Mother. She is bound, tortured, full of sores. Her tears run out of her eyes onto the earth and she cries out: "Behold and see if there be any sorrow like unto my sorrow."

23. *PICTURES FOR THE REDEMPTION OF THE GODDESS (3-29-1981)*

I dreamt that I had painted many pictures of the suffering Black Madonna. They were all heaped together. I was given to understand how important it was to paint these pictures for the redemption of the Goddess.

24. *I HAVE TO EAT THE BLACK MADONNA (4-4-1981)*

I dreamt that a batch of food was being prepared for me by someone unknown to me. That person held a dark ball or sphere in his or her hands. The sphere turned into a skull. The skull was called "The Black Madonna." That unknown person chopped the skull up and mixed it into some food for me. I was forced to eat that food.

25. *THE BLACK MADONNA ON TRIAL (5-11-1981)*

I dreamt of the Black Madonna and the Christ Child. Both were entirely black from head to toe. The mother stood on the left side, the boy on the right. They were both on trial. The issue was: are they both really part of the Godhead?

26. *THE EARTH CATHEDRAL IS BEING RESTORED (5-25-1981)*

I dreamt that I had arrived in an unknown city here in the United States. As I walked through a narrow, cobblestone street, I came to a huge ancient cathedral called "Our Lady of Guadeloupe." This cathedral had been built completely from red clay, was well constructed and rounded like a belly. The whole outside was painted with images of plants, trees, animals, and people in glowing earth colors. I especially remember the many reds and greens. That old church was a beautiful, soulful folk temple. I thought: "I have to show it to my German friends next time they come to the United States to visit me." I was just delighted to be able to show them something intrinsically North American that is fully equal to the best in European culture and can hold its own when compared to the cathedrals of Europe.

I entered the anteroom and saw that its walls and ceiling were painted with pictures in earth colors, just like the outside of the cathedral. High up on one wall I discovered a big painting of the Mother of God dressed in a flowing garment, a veil covering her head. Her arms were bare and full of sores. She was the suffering outcast, the leper woman. In her lap she held a cross with a crucified bleeding woman on it. This tortured woman was a Mother of God too. Before them knelt a third woman, much smaller than the suffering Mother of God, but she too was one.

I thought: "Aha! There she is."

Then I entered the round belly of the cathedral. It was as majestic as the Hagia Sophia in Istanbul, which it somewhat resembled. The lower half of the sanctuary was built several stories deep in the earth. The upper half reached several stories high above the ground. There were three windows in the apse's wall through which the light streamed into the belly of the church.

This cathedral was an ancient holy place of the people and was right now in the process of being restored. Throughout the cathedral I saw innumerable thick columns that reached from the dark floor to the ceiling high up into the light. Behind some of them I saw a raised platform with a few well-worn pews made from raw wood. Some peasants and a few pilgrims knelt there. When they spotted me, they smiled and waved.

The cathedral was totally empty. A gigantic rolled-up carpet leaned upright against the wall of the apse between the windows. It was handwoven in a thousand glowing shades of red into a pattern of a huge tree the branches of which were filled with blossoms, birds, and many animals. When the repairs were finished, the carpet would be hung in the apse on the wall as background for a huge painting of the Black Madonna.

27.   *THE SACRED CAVE OF THE BROTHERHOOD (6-13-1981)*

I dreamt that my analyst had given me the key to a secret cave high up in the mountains. He had described it to me and told me how to get there. Then he had sent me on a lonely quest to find it. This cave was one of many and a holy place since time immemorial. The North American Indians had known it for thousands of years. The entrance to the cave was well hidden behind trees and rocks. I reached it at the end of a very long journey and much hard work. When I found it, I recognized it at once.

No one could find the cave unless he or she was called. To find and enter it was a vocation. The secret had been passed on together with the key through the millennia from one solitary human being to another. Only a handful of people knew about its existence, since only once or twice in a century was someone called into the cave. The ones called to enter were in a mysterious way deeply connected to the spirits of those who had been here before. They met the essence of their elder brothers in the cave, since each person who had been here had left a gift for future generations.

The cave was large. It was dark on the left side and on the right side well lit by a light streaming down from above but originating in the earth itself. Bathed in that light I saw an ancient Native American blanket lying on the ground and on that blanket the gifts of those that had been here before. In the center stood a fairly large oval box. Around it had been placed pieces of finely woven fabric in earth colors, carvings of stone and wood, simple musical instruments, rocks and crystals, a book. I do not remember all the objects on that blanket, only that they all were sacred, earthy, simple, and homemade. I was deeply moved. I did not touch anything.

When I walked into the dark part of the cave, I found a big red brick fireplace built carefully into the wall. It was totally blackened by soot from much use.

When I had gone back into the light, I picked up the wooden oval box and opened it. In it I found the Holy of Holies, a white circular porous rock surrounded by a circle of feathers which had been stuck into it. Those feathers were half black and half white. The rock looked somewhat like a dried sponge. It had originated in a much wider context of life, had been broken off, placed in the box, and brought here. It contained the power of life.

My feeling was that it only needed to be immersed in water, which was its natural element, to come alive, sprout, and grow, because life itself was sleeping inside it. The feathered rock was something like an Indian medicine. I touched it reverently and a feeling of holiness came over me.

I was in a state of pure joy because I had come home. I belonged to this small band of spiritual brothers and felt tangibly connected to the essence of all who had been here before me. I felt their living presence all around me.

I took the feathered rock out of its box, held it in both hands, and contemplated it. Behind it I found a square, clear, standing mirror. This mirror was simultaneously the lid of the box protecting the rock. It also was a document of the brotherhood since it had inscribed on its surface the names of some brothers who had lived in the past two centuries and knew how to read and write. The brothers who had been here before that time had not been able to read or write. Three or four names were engraved on the mirror, also the dates 1782 or 1784. Each of the literate brothers had written one sentence about himself to be passed on to all those who would come to the cave. The illiterate ones had left the other gifts on the blanket: the essence and fruits of their life.

While I read the inscriptions, my husband and my son suddenly appeared at my side, peering over my shoulder. They desired to read what I was reading, but did not know how to decipher the messages or get their meaning. It bothered me to be distracted by them. I needed very much to be alone with what I had to do.

As suddenly as they had come, my husband and our son were gone again and I could continue to contemplate the legacy of my elder brothers. During my meditation I was given to understand that I too would have to deposit a sacred object on that blanket in the tradition of the brotherhood. The brothers coming after me would thus find my legacy preserved for them with the legacy of millennia.

I wondered what I possibly could give of myself that was worthy of being added to the sacred treasure. And so I stood in the cave lost in my own thoughts when the revelation hit me with the force of lightning.

The sacred object which I had to contribute was a painting of the Black Madonna. I saw it already finished on the blanket. It was tiny, but carefully worked. The Divine Face of the Goddess was deep black and emitted much sweetness, compassion, and grace. Her countenance, lit from within, radiated unearthly beauty in such a noble way that I was moved to tears.

The image then began to grow in stages until it was gigantic. I knew that I would have to go home to paint this picture and then return to the cave and bring it to the blanket. I knew I would have to use the best materials available to make it indestructible and permanent in every way.

I had the key to the cave. Any time I wanted to I could return to the cave to connect with the essence of my brothers and draw strength from them. I was separated from them only on the physical level by time. (When I woke up, I did not know if I had dreamt about "The Sacred Cave of the Brotherhood" or "The Cave of the Sacred Brotherhood".)

28. *THE FUSION OF BREAD AND WINE BY A SHAFT OF LIGHT (6-23-1981)*

I dreamt that my analyst sat at a table and I stood on his left side. Before him he had a gold chalice filled with red wine and a gold plate with a white host on it. He was contemplating the wine and the bread, wondering how they could be fused into a unity with the light from above without losing their own nature. He desperately wanted this to happen, but did not know how to go about it.

I knew the solution and told him that it was really simple. All we needed to do was to ask a master goldsmith to make a gold chalice with a small circular glass window in the bottom of the cup. This would permit the light from above to pass through the wine and then through the chalice and onto the host. The light would fuse bread and wine effortlessly together.

As I was speaking to my analyst, I saw the unification happen in front of our eyes: A beam of light fused bread and wine together with its own nature, by its own nature, and through its own nature into one.

29. *ACTIVE IMAGINATION: THE BIG BLACK MOTHER WITH LOVERS IN HER HAIR (7-21-1981)*

During active imagination I saw a big black woman whom I knew to be a mother. She was gigantic. On top of her head, I saw two people making love. They were as comfortable in her hair as if they were lying in a nest. The black woman had her hands crossed over her heart and her arms were filled with all kinds of warm-blooded animals that drank from her breasts. On her shoulders I saw all kinds of birds sitting and singing. On her body, around her navel, I saw all kinds of small insects and cold-blooded animals like frogs, lizards, turtles, and dragonflies which were happily enjoying their life and their closeness to her. Around the big black woman I saw living branches like a halo of plants, bushes, and trees in bloom.

30. *THE BLACK MADONNA LOOKS AT ME (8-13-1981)*

I dreamt of the Black Madonna. She was sitting at a table and many people were with her. The scene was like with Jesus at the Last Supper. She was very black and she also wore a black garment, the end of which she had put over her head as a veil. The garment had a wide orange-yellow border. Her dark face had an unearthly beauty; it radiated transcendence. She looked at me and I liked it.

31. *THE HANDS OF THE BLACK MADONNA, THE CREATOR (8-31-1981)*

I woke up in the middle of the night and saw two big black hands in front of me.
They were the hands of the Black Madonna. She was squatting or sitting on the earth
and shaping all kinds of things out of the earth into lovely living shapes. She made
birds and flowers that throbbed with life. She also created sculptures of human beings
out of the earth and they turned into warm living beings. Her hands were working
right in front of me. I saw them as if I were sitting in her lap, leaning against her
heart. The hands were as big as if I were a small child looking at the hands of the
mother. These hands were dark and very fine and sensitive and beautiful. I kept
thinking: "She is the Great Creator."

32. *THE SIXTEEN DISGUISES OF THE BLACK MADONNA (9-19-1981)*

I dreamt that I saw a black figure in front of me. This person was completely
wrapped in black and the head was covered with an executioner's hood. There were
no round openings for the eyes but there were two tiny slits made from silk. The figure
underneath this horrible costume was alive and laughed loudly. Someone said: "That
is my mother." Then the woman pulled the black henchman's hood off her head and
out came the most horrible skull with some decomposed and moldy flesh still clinging
to it. The woman started to turn ever so slowly. It was a terrible sight. Then the face
started to change into a living face. It came alive and finally transformed itself into
the lovely face of a young woman. She smiled kindly. A voice said something like
"sixteen envelopes" and meant sixteen disguises or veils.

   The woman took me by the hands and danced with me an elegant and lovely
dance. She was wearing a long black garment.

   I said to myself: "I will remain European, this is not part of my culture. I will keep
my long blue skirt and walking shoes. I will remain faithful to my own cultural
heritage."

33. *I SEW LITURGICAL VESTMENTS FOR THE PRIESTESSES OF THE BLACK MADONNA
     (10-1-1981)*

I dreamed I measured Catholic liturgical vestments in order to sew new vestments
myself. But the one I was making was meant to be worn by women in the service of
the Black Madonna. Therefore I made my vestment 70 cm longer than the traditional
ones, so that its proportions would be elegant and the lines flowing. The color had to
be green and the fabric pure silk. The material and everything connected with it had
to come from an unspoiled, natural source. I planned to add precious embroidery,
like had never been done before. The priestess of the Black Madonna would wear
this robe while saying mass in honor of God the Mother.

   Then I discovered that hair grew out of my fingertips. I thought this strange, but
accepted it. The same thing happened to my sister. The hair made our hands very
sensitive.

34. *THE CRYSTAL WITH THE FIERY HEART INSIDE (5-7-1982)*

I dreamt I threw myself with all my power onto the earth, or maybe I was pulled
down by gravity somehow and surrendered. I fell on my knees in adoration. The
earth was black and green grass grew out of it. And when I was on my knees and
real close to the earth, I saw a clear crystal in front of me that was round and
many-faceted. Inside of the crystal was a fiery red heart.

35. *THE EARTH CATHEDRAL IS FINISHED (4-29-1983)*

I dreamt that I stood with a friend on a bridge in the mountains leading across a
river. We heard many voices singing ancient and very moving songs in honor of the
Blessed Mother. When I looked down from the bridge, a big ship filled with pilgrims
came from the left, crossing underneath the bridge, carried by the waves towards the

right. The pilgrims all sang in harmony together and the beauty of their chants affected me deeply.

The bridge I stood on was at the same time a street leading into a forest on top of the closest mountain. No one was permitted to drive there by car. It was holy ground and one had to walk by foot. Over the treetops rose the round dome of a huge cathedral and next to it the top of a huge freestanding column. Both were painted with strangely interlocking black and white shapes. There was more black than white there, but everything was harmoniously balanced. This was the completed sanctuary of the Black Madonna, where I had to go.

36. *THE CONJUNCTIO (7-1-1983)*

I dreamt that I saw in a preview or prophetic vision three stars in the sky linking up into a conjunction.

Then I dreamt a second dream. In this dream the vision of the previous one became reality. I was standing together with my husband in the fields near the city. Grain, fruits, vegetables, and everything else in those fields were ripe for the harvest. It was in the middle of the day, but the sky was twilight blue. We saw the sun, the moon, and many stars moving in some kind of dance around each other in the sky. A voice said that the "Great Conjunction" would take place, a rare and unusual thing which happens only once every few thousand years. We would see it and be its witnesses.

And so we were waiting with great expectation to see if what the voice had announced would really come true. Sun, moon, and stars were still revolving around each other in the sky and nothing happened for quite some time. Suddenly the three "great" stars joined up horizontally: the sun on the left, Mercury in the center, and the moon on the right. Mysterious signs were written with light into them. Sun, moon, and Mercury touched each other. They glowed with an inner light. While the sun, moon, and Mercury stayed together, the "lesser" stars kept dancing in the sky. For a long time it was not at all certain that the "Great Conjunction" would really take place.

But all of a sudden it happened, and the emotions that swept through me were utter amazement and gratitude for being allowed to witness this miracle of nature. I saw that the seven planets lined up vertically under Mercury according to size. Sun, moon, and Mercury looked quite large, while the planets seemed much smaller. But all glowed from within and had those strange signs written into them with light. The completed constellation of the "Great Conjunction" looked like the Greek letter, tau.

Upon awakening, I realized immediately that the strange word Cõquecoi of dream No. 2 had been a garbled version of the word Conjunctio.

37. *ACTIVE IMAGINATION: THE BLACK MADONNA SPEAKS TO ME ABOUT MY MOTHER (3-18-84)*

During active imagination I talked to the Black Madonna about my sad childhood, the miseries of my life, and my at times unbearable longing for mother love. I had been going over my first childhood dream, realizing for the first time that it had been a good and helpful dream. I asked the Black Madonna if she could see any meaning in the suffering of the child. She was silent for a long time, Suddenly she spoke to me about my mother:

SHE WAS JUST THE POT I COOKED MY SOUP IN.
SHE WAS JUST THE RAG I WRAPPED MY DIAMOND IN.
SHE WAS JUST THE SHARD THAT I GREW MY LUMINOUS ROSE IN.

38. *I AM GIVEN A NEW NAME: TA DAYA WADO (11-16-1984)*

I dreamt that a black woman embraced me from the back, hugging my behind and honoring it. She massaged it and worked on it lovingly. It felt good and I said to her: "This is the best behind hug I ever received."

When she was finished, I had a new name: Ta Daya Wado.
This was a North American Indian name, signifying my new life.

39.   *I FIGHT FOR THE ASSUMPTION OF MARY (11-18-1984)*

I dreamt that I was a Catholic nun and sitting at a conference table with some other nuns and priests. The Holy Father had just sent an important letter about the Assumption of Mary to all religious communities. We were supposed to read it. But instead of being printed on paper, the Papal letter was written on huge white women's girdles complete with garters. The older nuns and priests accepted these girdles in unquestioning obedience. But I refused to take it and yelled: "The message of the Assumption of Mary is so precious that it must be printed in the form of a book! And it has to be a beautiful book." Everyone was shocked and stunned that I dared to speak out against tradition. But I got even angrier and screamed: "If this is not changed and the message remains written on girdles, I will see to it that the Bible is written on longjohns."

They all became terribly upset and did not know what to do. They did not really object to the stupid girdles because they were so used to them they did not know the difference. But what they could not come to terms with was my anger. And so they did the usual, they tried to silence me through shunning. One by one they left the room.

Suddenly a handsome man resembling the singer Julio Iglesias tried to seduce me. I screamed at him: "How much substance do you have?" And by this I meant his humanity and his integrity. He reached into his pocket, pulled out his money and showed it to me on his outstretched hand: two nickels. I became very impatient and kept yelling, but he did not seem to get the message.

By now the nuns and priests had returned and were trying to sway me through verbal criticism of my stubbornness. I did not even give them an answer because I was fully aware of the hopelessness of my situation. I threw myself on the ground and touched the earth with my forehead. I remained kneeling in this position for a very long time.

But then a fellow nun with a humble and sad face came up to me. In her features I could read her past. She had spent it in the service of the church. It consisted of nothing but loneliness, hard work, much obedience, and a lot of silent suffering. And now came the real temptation because this nun asked me in a quiet and humble voice to do her a favor. In order to restore the peace, she asked me as a special favor to her to sign a formal apology for upsetting the ordinary course of things, for disobeying traditions, and for daring to oppose the priests.

In a loud and clear voice I simply said: "No, I will not sign the form. I cannot act in any other way than I acted because the hand of God has touched me."

Again I touched the Earth with my forehead in adoration and remained that way on my knees, paying no attention to the commotion around me.

40.   *SINGING THE PRAISES OF THE BLACK MADONNA (11-25-1984)*

I dreamt that I held my bowed psaltery in my hands. I made music for the Black Madonna. Together with many other women, I sang her praises.

41.   *A TREE GROWS OUT OF A BLACK POOL IN THE CHURCH (12-25-1984)*

I dreamt that I attended mass in a church where I had not been before. My place was in the back where the pews stood on higher ground so that everyone could see the mass being celebrated in front. Two masses took place in the church. I attended both. The first one I attended with my husband but the second one I attended alone.

The mass was celebrated by a priestess. She read the holy words of transformation from a big book on a handcarved lectern. There was no altar. In its place I saw a circular black pool out of which grew a tree that touched the ceiling. It was blooming. Many small white blossoms shone in its rich green foliage. A light that had no outer source illuminated the tree and I could see it reflected in the waters of the pool.

When it was time for Holy Communion, I remained in my pew and contemplated the tree in the pool instead of joining the others. I had gone to communion with my husband during the first mass.

And so, remaining by myself, I wrote in my dream journal what I saw in order to have a record of it. And before me, in the rack of the pew, where the Bible, prayer books, and hymnals are usually kept, I found a whole stack of my dream journals instead.

42. MY VERY OWN HOLY BOOK (2-19-1988)

I dreamt that I was sorting out my belongings since I had to move. I packed my most precious possessions into a suitcase.

The one thing that had to be preserved at all cost and under all circumstances was my very own Holy Book. It was imperative that I carry it with me at all times.

I had made it myself, covered it with precious old linen, and printed on the outside that this was my Bible. Into the book I had put pictures of the most important and memorable events of my life. These were photographs in highly contrasting blacks and whites which I had taken with a small, primitive, homemade camera. I had then spent much time adding colors and shaping the pictures into simple works of art. Finally I had added some writing.

The book's center section consisted of a sequence of images which had captured a most important memory of mine, namely the exact moment when a human being had made it across an inlet of the ocean to the other side. I had caught on my film that lovely summer day, the flowering prairie, the rocks on the edge of the water, the tall green reeds, the purity and innocence of the land. But most of all, I had captured the scene of that human being completing her jump, and doing it in a simple and manageable fashion. I had also photographed a quarry in which perfect stone cubes were piled up and then spread out along the shore one by one.

I had photographed all of these objects because I loved their simple beauty and their rhythm. They were really just things that are always all around us and can be found anywhere. No one else had paid attention to them. But for me they had taken on a personal meaning which was irreplaceable and had to be saved at all cost. The reason was: No other human being would see them ever again in the same way.

That book was the most important thing in my life and I loved it with my whole being.

43. I AM A SHAMAN OF THE BLACK MADONNA (5-1-1988)

I dreamt that I was standing at a railroad station. By the tracks lay the opened suitcases of prisoners. They were condemned men who would be put away on the next train. A judge recited a list of their crimes and read them their sentences. I knew two of the men. Their offense was that they were shamans. And their crimes were that instead of being just like everyone else and conforming to ordinary standards, they had turned things around. They had venerated the life force and served life in a way opposite to what is customary. And worst of all, they had worshipped the Black Madonna and angels that had black skin instead of white.

One of the condemned men was a friend of mine whom I had known well for quite some time. The court had taken all his shamanic tools away: his drum, the beater, his rattle, click sticks, bandana, the candle, his abalone shell, even the sage, cedar, and sweetgrass. And so he was stripped of all outer possibilities to do his work.

When he saw me, he whispered to me that he needed some money. The first thing he wanted to do after his arrival in the prison camp was to buy for himself a shaman's ring: a slender gold band, which is the one basic thing that a shaman needs to do his work. I was wearing just such a slim gold ring on the ring finger of my right hand. On my left hand I wore my wedding band as usual. I whispered back to him: "I will give you that ring now before you leave because I have one for you at home." And by saying that I acknowledged consciously for the first time in my life that I, too, was a shaman.

All I had to do was to go home and get that ring for him, because I kept three golden shaman's rings in my house. Two of them I would add to the other rings on my hands. And one in the shape of an octagon I would give away to my friend. From now on I would wear my three shaman rings together with the wedding band forever.

When my friend understood that I would give him what he needed right away, he recognized me as a fellow shaman and a deep bonding took place.

My husband and I immediately went to get the rings. Between us walked a little girl with long blond hair, holding both of us by the hands. Very suddenly evening came and it was dark around us. We reached an intersection, a real crossroad. All four corners had red traffic lights and the traffic could not flow. We could not cross. So we simply waited until all four lights changed to green. Now we were free to cross the street. But a moment later I realized that all the lights had gone out. They were not needed because daylight had returned. Everyone looked out for himself and the traffic. Each person took the full responsibility for what he or she was doing. Everyone and everything moved smoothly. We had just reached the center of the intersection when a voice said: "The war is over."

44. *ACTIVE IMAGINATION: THE BLACK MADONNA ASCENDS FROM UNDERNEATH CHICAGO AND IS FREE (8-27-1988)*

During active imagination which was part of a solitary pipe ceremony that I did in the early morning hours before my earth altar, I saw the Black Madonna imprisoned in the dungeon underneath the city of Chicago. She suffered terribly. I reached that depth of agony where she was so that I could be with her. Everything there was darkness, pain, sorrow, despair, emptiness, desolation, abandonment, hopelessness, and utter hell. I suffered and wept with her.

Suddenly the earth above us split open in the shape of an even-armed cross and light streamed in. She ascended. She did not have to shatter the concrete and asphalt of Chicago in a big explosion of rage. A channel for all that imprisoned and neglected energy from deep within the earth opened up because the Black Madonna was given time and attention in ceremony.

She felt loved, honored, and cherished as I made tobacco ties, burned sage, cedar, and sweetgrass, drummed and sang, smoked the sacred pipe for all my relations, remembered the dreams and contemplated them, dreamt them onward by doing active imagination, and went inward to be with her. And so she came out of the prison. The breakthrough has happened. She finally can breathe freely, walk in the flowering prairies and all over the earth, in the forests, and in all lands. She can glorify herself in the dreams and hearts of the people.

She was extremely glad to be free. She smiled at me while her face was still wet with tears.

45. *ACTIVE IMAGINATION: THE GOLDEN TIPI OF RECONCILIATION (8-27-1988)*

That same evening I did active imagination again during a ceremony with a woman friend. We sat at the shore of Lake Michigan together on boulders which lay in a circle. We had lit a fire in the center. We were drumming. It was late in the evening and the full moon rose over the lake. The waves were coming in and it felt as if they were rocking us.

When I did active imagination, I suddenly saw us drumming inside of a large tipi. A fire, safely surrounded by rocks, burned strongly in its center. Then all of a sudden I found myself outside again and alone in the darkness. From a distance I contemplated the tipi which glowed and shone from within like pure and living gold. A huge golden eagle, metaphor for the Transcendent, the Great Mystery of our existence, plus many other animals symbolizing our interconnectedness with all life forms were painted on it in gold. In an instant I was again inside the tipi. The fire *illuminated a huge picture of the Black Madonna painted in the very same spot inside as the Great Mystery outside. She was surrounded by golden flowers, golden trees, golden animals, golden crystals and rocks. People of all colors, races, creeds, and nationalities came to her from both sides, and all were golden-hued.*

This was the Sacred Golden Tipi of Reconciliation. This was an Earth Cathedral in the prairies.

Four days later I saw the Black Madonna standing in a blooming prairie in full daylight. She was huge. She lovingly watched over and protected the Golden Tipi of Reconciliation. Then she lay down on the earth among the flowers and the animals, and the Sacred Golden Tipi of Reconciliation stood upon her heart like a small golden tent.

46. I AM A PRIESTESS OF THE BLACK MADONNA (12-29-1988)

I dreamt that I went to a Catholic church and knelt down in a dark corner way in the back. All I wanted to do was just to pray for a little while and remain unseen in the back, where no one would pay any attention to me. I did not want to be seen, because I wore the flowing red robe of a priestess made of fine, thin silk. Being naked underneath it, I feared my body would show through the almost transparent weave. The robe glowed in all the colors of the rainbow and was simultaneously red, like a red-hued rainbow.

Suddenly my analyst walked into the church, saw me, and asked what I was doing in that dark corner so far in the back of the church. I said that I had come to attend the mass and planned to stay in the dark corner for protection. He said: "No way! You come with me. I will show you your place."

My analyst was a priest and wore the same liturgical vestments as I. He too looked like a red-hued rainbow. It was the most beautiful priestly robe imaginable, very comfortable too, wide and flowing, and handmade from the most exquisite silk. It ended in a wine-red border.

My analyst and I were priest and priestess in the same church. He took my hand and made me walk with him through the center aisle and towards the altar. And there in front of everyone was a place for me already prepared on the far right side.

I felt like a colorful red bird among all the folks in the church who were dressed normally. But by now I felt more comfortable and safer because I wore a snow white cotton shift underneath the vestment. I also had a pair of simple sandals on my feet, the tops of which looked like two red-hued rainbows.

The mass began and soon it was time for Holy Communion. I went up some steps and knelt down on the black marble in front of the altar. Many people knelt down with me. Because I had not been in any church for decades, I was not used to kneeling and slid a bit. But I soon adjusted.

When it was my turn to receive communion, the priest did the usual thing and held up the gold chalice and the host for me. But suddenly to my utter surprise a small red kernel of candy-covered popcorn jumped out of his mouth into my hands which held a bundle of keys. It was his own holy communion, which he had just taken for himself during the mass. I was surprised because he put a host into everyone else's mouth.

The priest just smiled at me, and I went back to my place carrying this body of Christ in my hands. There I knelt down and gave myself communion by eating the sweet, red kernel.

47. ACTIVE IMAGINATION: THE BLACK MADONNA, WHITE BUFFALO WOMAN, THE KWAN YIN, AND THE SHEKINAH HAVE COME TO HEAL THE EARTH (4-13-1989)

During active imagination I saw the Black Madonna coming from the West, White Buffalo Woman from the North, the Kwan Yin from the South, and the Shekinah from the East. They were standing on golden clouds watching over the earth. When they had come real close to our planet, they stretched their hands out and created a sacred energy field around it. Each of the Goddesses held one of her hands underneath the Earth and her other hand above it. Their hands and the clouds linked up. The planet hovered in the center. And they blessed and healed the suffering Earth.

48.   *THE BLACK MADONNA'S DRUM AND MY DRUM ARE CONNECTED (4-26-1989)*

I dreamt that I was doing active imagination and filling myself up with energy to do inner work. A dark woman was at my right side, almost like a shadow, filling me with Divine energy. Somehow we did this together so that the healing energy could stream from her into me and through me to others. This happened during the night. Her big drum and my little drum lay side by side on the ground. I saw them mysteriously connected in the gentle light of the night.

49.   *THE BLACK MADONNA HEALS ME AND MANY OTHER PEOPLE WITH HER VEIL*
       (5-4-1989)

I dreamt that I was lying on the earth. The Black Madonna knelt next to me and took one end of her white veil into her hands and put it on me and many other people for healing. She covered me with it, wrapped it over me, and swaddled me in it. Her hands were so very gentle. She smiled.

50.   *THE CHRIST CHILD, WHICH IS THE BLACK MADONNA AS A LITTLE GIRL*
       (9-28-1989)

For a month I incubated dreams about the role of the transpersonal psyche in my life and work. I wanted to know as much as I possibly could about the relationship between ego and Self. And I wanted to hear what the unconscious had to say about it. I even incubated dreams to check whether I had understood correctly the dreams that had been given to me. Finally I used the incubation phrase: "What does the transpersonal psyche want from me?" I dreamt the following dream.

I dreamt that I sat in a room together with a small group of people. An Inca had come from South America and brought with him the life-size statue of a woman saint made from totally clear rock crystal. This saint was an Indian holy woman from the Andes Mountains who had spent her life like Saint Francis of Assisi: loving and caring for all of life, being utterly in love with the Earth and the Cosmos. The Inca was going to talk to us about her life.

We were all sitting cross-legged on the ground; to my right sat a young North American Indian woman. The Inca had now finished his talk and began to show us something wonderful. He had brought to us a most sacred, most beloved small ancient statue. It was the image of a holy child, the Native American equivalent of the Christ Child. But it was a little girl of about three and a half years with a dark face. It was a little Black Madonna. She stood on a thick square slab of wood representing the earth. The face and body of the little girl were the core of the statue: they had been carved in one piece from wood and were the most ancient part of the image and quite weathered. This core was dressed or rather wrapped in colorful pieces of handwoven woolen cloth with folk patterns in a symphony of reds. The clothes had been renewed many times over the centuries as needed. The Holy Child wore tiny sandals. She had her own little cooking pots and frying pans. There even was a flat round black obsidian by her little feet, representing her very own pool of water or well. She had a little red rainbow-hued carrying blanket. And I think she had her own small weaving loom.

This was a most sacred image from a place of pilgrimage located high in the Andes Mountains. It had been venerated by the Indians since the sixteenth century. Innumerable people had prayed before it. They had poured their souls out to it, their dreams of deliverance, their tears, their sufferings, their helplessness and despair, but also their love and their smiles.

And now it was here with us in North America. The Inca handed the little Black Madonna to the young Indian woman next to me. He told her to hold the sacred image, love it, rock it, kiss it, and play with it, as if the Christ Child were alive. And she did that.

Then the Inca spoke to me and said that since I am not Indian, I was not permitted the same intimacy with the sacred image, but that I would be allowed to hold and venerate it later. And so, when the young woman had played with the little Black Madonna to her heart's content, she gave her to me.

It was a great honor to hold the Divine Child in my hands. I contemplated her in silence for a long time. Then I looked at her from all sides, turning her around and around in my hands to take in all the details consciously. Every time I discovered something that I had not been aware of before, I shared it with my friend, who delighted in everything with me. The very last part of the image that caught my attention was the thick wooden block underneath the feet of the Holy Little Girl. It was charred and blackened by soot from the many candles which the people had lit in front of the statue over the course of centuries. When I was finished, I handed the Sacred Child back to my young neighbor.

Then the wonderfully clear crystal statue of the sacred woman from the mountains, who had lived like Saint Francis, captured my attention again. She had in the meantime been elevated and stood much higher now on a beautifully handcarved pedestal. Stillness surrounded us as I contemplated her with my Native American friend.

51. I HAVE TO CONTEMPLATE MY DEATH (11-12-1989)

I dreamt that I had to contemplate my death and prepare myself for it. Every day I would have to think about it and give time to this important matter.

Then I dreamt that I was in a church. I sang the Gregorian chant "Dies Irae" from the Catholic Mass of the Dead. A requiem mass was being celebrated for someone who had died and lay in an open casket before the altar. I walked over to the coffin to take a look at the corpse and saw that it was me. Then the dream shifted. I found myself in a kitchen cooking food for many people. This was the work that I had to do.

52. THE BLACK WHALE TEACHES ME HOW TO DRUM (11-12-1989)

I dreamt a third dream that same night. In it I stood at the shore of the ocean next to a big black whale. The whale had come to the coast on purpose and beached herself so she could be near me and teach me how to use my shaman's drum. She longed to bridge the gap between the ocean and the land, between the whales and us humans. So she now lay on her belly next to me and looking me straight in the eye, she taught me how to beat my drum to comfort and heal the people: she slowly and deliberately moved her tail back and forth in a simple rhythm. The earth was her drum and her tail the drum stick: with each stroke she touched the earth. When I had absorbed the rhythm and memorized it for future use, many people came running towards us from all sides. They helped me push the whale back into deep water. She swam away joyfully.

53. MY ANCESTOR, THE SIBERIAN SHAMAN, PASSES HIS POWER ON TO ME (11-12-1989)

I had a fourth dream and dreamt that the city had just sworn me in as their police chief when an outlaw called me long distance on the telephone. He was a villain and thief who together with other male grave robbers had just discovered the burial site of one of my ancestors in Northern Siberia. When they had dug up the grave they found next to the decomposed body an ancient shaman's drum. It was made from deerskin, much worn and blackened from the passage of time. Since the grave robbers did not know what to do with it, they had decided to contact me. In an instant I was in Siberia to take a look at things. The drum was still usable and I claimed it for myself. Then I was back in the United States. After a while the outlaw called me up again. Now they had found an ancient red abalone shell in the grave and did not know what it was for. But I knew, of course, that it was meant to burn herbs in for cleansing during shamanic work. A moment later I was at the grave site and claimed it for myself. In the next instant I found myself back here in America. As they dug deeper and deeper, the villains found more and more shamanic ritual objects in the ground. Each time they did not know what to make of them; each time they telephoned me; each time I went to Siberia; each time I claimed for myself what once belonged to my ancestor; and each time I brought these treasures with me to the United States.

In this way my Siberian ancestor transferred his power on to me. Although he had passed on a long time ago, his spirit was in a mysterious way alive in the here and now. He rejoiced that the shaman's bloodline had not died out with him, but that the gift had surfaced in me and that I would continue the work. I loved and treasured his legacy. All those sacred ceremonial objects, those objects that had once belonged to him and were now mine, delighted my heart.

54.   *ACTIVE IMAGINATION: I RECEIVE THE LEGACY OF MY SHAMAN ANCESTRESS, SOPHIA (11-12-1989)*

I was so awed by these dreams that I wanted to know more and did active imagination. I met the spirit of my shaman ancestor and he took me with him to his big family tent somewhere in the Russian Arctic. It was fashioned from black bear hides. The air was crystal clear. Snowflakes drifted down from the clouds and settled like tiny stars on the black fur of the tent. It now looked as if it was made from a piece of the starry night sky.

The tent was clean and comfortable to live in. In its center burned a nice big fire. Smoke rose straight up from it and passed through the smoke hole to the clouds. We sat down and my ancestor told me, that he had a wife who also had been a shaman. He and his wife had supported each other spiritually and helped one another in their work to advise, console, and heal the people. But when she died, she was not buried next to him. Her grave was located on a distant mountain where her own helping spirits dwelt.

Before she passed over, Sophia had known through the spirits that I would come. She had seen me in a vision before her death and known that I would find her grave and that I would continue the shamanic tradition. She prepared a box with an inheritance for me and insisted that it must be buried with her. Her last thoughts had been of me. She had blessed me in the knowledge that some day I would come and claim her legacy for myself.

I now saw that small black iron chest from Sophia's grave standing on my earth altar here in my home in the United States. After I had saged myself and it, I broke the lock and lifted the cover. The chest held two golden cubes each the size of two fists. But when I opened them, they were empty.

I understood immediately: one of them had been filled with Sophia's breath and the other with her husband's. She had had these cubes fashioned from pure gold and then simply breathed into one. Then she had sealed it. Her husband had breathed into the second golden cube and she had sealed that one too. As I had opened the boxes, their breaths had flown out and I had inhaled them. She had foreseen this and had wished this to happen. By carefully planning my inheritance, she had created a living bridge between me and herself and her husband, connecting me to that uninterrupted chain of Siberian shamans stretching through the millennia and from ancient Siberia to modern-day America.

55.   *MY SHAMAN ANCESTOR TEACHES ME (11-12-1989)*

I had a fifth dream that same night. I dreamt that my Siberian shaman ancestor was transmitting his knowledge to me. He taught me, standing next to the sink in my kitchen, while I held a carton with twelve white eggs in my hands.

56. I CHARGE MYSELF WITH BLACK MADONNA ENERGY (11-18-1989)

I dreamt that I stood at the foot of a hill where the Black Madonna worked her miracles as she was wandering across the earth. A woman friend was at my side and I pointed out a round spot of black soil to her. It was the point where I could plug into the earth and charge myself up to do shamanic work. It was pure Black Madonna energy.

57. THE HUGE BEAR WITH THE BLACK BLESSING HANDS WANTS TO BE SET FREE (11-27-1989)

I dreamt of a huge bear who was pleading her case in court. She was on trial about her future. I was in the courtroom and saw her from behind. Her coat was reddish brown. Her front paws, which looked like human hands, were black. The bear stood upright on her hind legs and walked like a human being. She could sign with her hands and was talking in American Sign Language. She was demanding to be given her freedom. She longed to be set free and walk among the people unrestrained. Then she raised her hands in the traditional Jewish gesture of blessing.

I was scared of the bear's great powers. The responsible people too felt that she should not be given her freedom. After all she was a bear with a bear nature and the habits of bears and a danger to ordinary folks.

Then the dream shifted. I found myself in a place adjacent to the courtroom. It was a dark room in the shape of a perfect cube. Next to me stood a woman who was sick and tired of the whole trial and demanded justice for the bear. Between us and the courtroom was a closed and bolted wooden door with a glass window in it. I saw that the bear was looking through that window at me. She was pushing against the door wanting to be let in and be with me. The dead-bolt lock on my side had a bar connected to it. The woman who was with me in the room reached for it to open the door for the bear. But I rushed over to prevent that. She now was pushing from one direction to open the door and I was pushing from the opposite direction to keep it locked. I screamed at her: "Well, it's either you or me!" And although she was strong and almost succeeded, I was stronger and beat her. The door stayed locked.

The dream shifted again and I was back in the courtroom next to a children's carriage with a little girl in it. She was about three and a half years old, unkempt and wore dirty and ragged clothes. Her hair was shaggy and neglected. She looked like a little Tibetan peasant child or maybe Siberian or Eskimo. Her face was round like the moon with Mongolian features and slanted eyes. A man took care of her. The bear loved that little girl and was gentle and tame around her because they were friends and loved each other. Then I saw that the little girl had laid a smelly turd right smack in the middle of the pillow for her head. I then became aware of how healthy, robust, strong, and happy that child was.

Again the dream shifted and I found myself in a lovely garden. I stood under a tree the nature of which was to bear the most exquisite blossoms and fruits in summer and then to be regular for the rest of the year. This was possible because this tree was really made from two trees: a branch from a precious fruit tree had once been grafted onto a regular basswood tree. I now was standing under that big tree with the man who had taken care of the child. And the bear was with us and she was free. The bear knew the secret of how to transform an ordinary shade-giving tree into a precious fruit-bearing tree. We had taken the bear along with us to learn that secret from her. And she was teaching us. Part of the secret was that the ordinary tree had to be shrouded in a white burial cloth when the time was right for the transformation into a fruit-bearing tree. The bear alone knew the whole secret and she was teaching it to us.

58. *THE BEAR WITH THE BLESSING HANDS OFFERS ME A WELL (12-2-1989)*

   I dreamt I stood at a wall or window sill that reached to my eye level. From the other side the big bear with the black blessing hands came towards me. She reached over the wall. In her hands she held a well: a long, deep well that could be set into the ground to reach the water. She offered it to me.

59. *THE MISSAL OF THE BLACK MADONNA (4-15-1990)*

   I dreamt I was binding a big book: the Missal of the Black Madonna. I was binding it in lovely night-sky-blue silk and was in the process of gluing the corners down.

60. *THE CHANNEL OF LIGHT INSIDE OF THE EARTH (4-17-1990)*

   I dreamt of a long channel of light that reached deep down into the earth. There was blackness on the left and blackness on the right. But the channel of light was in the center. I was inside it and would go down, then up, then down, then up again. I could move freely in it.

61. *A CATHEDRAL FOR THE WHOLE PLANET (6-8-1990)*

   I dreamt that a cathedral would be built in the city where I live. It was going to be big enough for the whole world to fit in it, that is, planet Earth would actually fit in that cathedral. In the dream I had a vision in which I saw the cathedral finished and the earth filled it from wall to wall and from floor to ceiling.

   The building plans were ready. The only thing left to do was the actual physical building. People all over were feverishly training and preparing themselves for the hands-on work of raising the cathedral. People everywhere knew about the coming work and longed to be a masterly part of it.

   The pope was still debating it and could not reach a decision.

   I felt myself somehow pushed towards this cathedral. Very aware of what was happening, I said to my husband: "And to think of it, that the Black Madonna let us settle in this city so many years ago, and that we will be a part of all of this."

62. *ATAHUALPA MAKES ALTARS OF THE BLACK MADONNA (9-13-1991)*

   I dreamt I saw Atahualpa in his workshop. He was swinging an ax and hewing planks from a tree for altars, pictures, and frames. Through the flying chips I saw a finished altar at the back wall. It was the size of a regular table. Right in its center stood a square icon of the Black Madonna in the rose garden. On a night-blue background all around her were specks of pure gold, the stars.

   Atahualpa had only a single tool to work with, his ax. With it he did everything, no matter how difficult or delicate. When things turned out rough or uneven, he would patiently smooth them with the tip of his ax until they were wonderfully even and as polished as can be. He was smoothing, smoothing, smoothing . . .
[Note: Atahualpa is said to have been the last Inca ruler to have been murdered by Pizarro.]

63. *WITH C. G. JUNG IN THE PROTESTANT EARTH CHAPEL (10-13-1991)*

   I dreamt I was sitting together with a companion in a Protestant chapel in Switzerland across from C. G. Jung. He was talking to me. The chapel was completely empty; even the stone altar in the front was bare. But there was a magnificent square panel on the ceiling divided by a cross into four smaller panels, each a colorful and finely worked piece of art. The one farthest to the right showed a picture of planet Earth as seen from space, surrounded by the stars of the milky way. While C. G. Jung was speaking, I contemplated this image through a large transparent camera filter in the color of golden amber. The Earth appeared golden-hued to me. When C. G. Jung had finished speaking, that filter was mine to keep. Suddenly I saw a huge "Earthkeeper" crystal filled with rainbows in my arms.

64. *FOUR NAKED WOMEN CARRY THE EARTH INTO THE CHURCH (1-30-1992)*

I dreamt I was painting a picture and looked into it and through it to the other side as through a window. There I saw four naked women walking together. They had their arms raised high and with their outstretched hands they held the whole Earth up and carried it. They were simple human beings like you and me.

When in active imagination I dreamt the dream onward, I saw the women carry the Earth into the church, boldly walking up the center aisle towards the altar.

65. *THE PEOPLE PULL EACH OTHER TO SAFETY (2-15-1992)*

I dreamt that it was night and I stood on the banks of a dark cold river. There were many people in the water. They were all caught in the dangerous and freezing stream. But they all helped each other to safety. A mother in a heavy coat pulled her little girl by the hands. I saw the child's legs in handknit brown stockings and leather shoes glide through the water. The mother in turn was pulled by a man in a streetcoat, her husband. Everyone reached out and saved another human being. They pulled one another out from darkness, fear, and isolation into the warmth and hope of human connectedness. They did this by touching one another, holding on to each other, and not letting go, no matter what. They realized that they only had each other. That was what saved them. It made them act swiftly, instinctively and decisively. And so each person did what had to be done. They all used their hands to hold and help. They knew they were one family.

66. *THE GOLDEN BIRD HAS LANDED (3-8-1992)*

I dreamt a big golden bird with absolutely huge golden wings landed right in front of me on the ground. For a moment her wings still hovered in the air. Then they folded down.

67. *THE ICON OF THE BLACK MADONNA SAVES THE PEOPLE (4-10-1992)*

I dreamt I saw a dark river from above. Looking down on it I saw a Russian icon of the Black Madonna as big as a raft floating face up on the choppy waves. It swam there so that the people who were lost in the water could reach for it, grab it, hold on to it, climb up onto it, and be carried by it to safety.

68. *I HAVE A CHRISTIAN, A JEWISH, AND A SHAMANIC ALTAR (4-19-1992)*

I dreamt I saw three plain wooden tables in a room. They were my altars standing in a half circle, touching each other. One of them was Christian, one was Jewish, and one was a shaman's altar. All three of them protected each other so they all could flourish equally well. They were there for the healing of the body, mind, and soul of the people.

The Christian altar was full of burning candles. Two of those had been transferred to the Jewish altar. And one of them would go on the shaman's altar. In this way the shamanic altar was being received into the protection of the strong ones. Because protection went out from the Christian altar to the Jewish one, and then from both of them to the shaman's altar.

69. *A FORCE PUSHES ME TO AN ALTAR (6-7-1992)*

I dreamt I was standing before a simple wooden table, the boards of which were quite weathered. All kinds of lovely ripe fruits were piled high on it. I took a cantaloupe and changed it into something holy. At this moment a great flash of light happened inside of me and began to radiate outward.

A shift took place and I was with some people. We were just standing around when a force grabbed me from behind and with one hard push shoved me towards an altar. I saw that it was a stone altar like in a church, covered with a white linen cloth. The altar was empty. I wore priestly vestments.

70. *I AM VULNERABLE TO THE UNIVERSE (6-17-1992)*

  I dreamt I was walking down a path under the open night sky filled with stars. I was drumming on my shaman's drum. I was naked except for my prayer shawl, which I wore around my shoulders and knotted over my chest, so that my backside was covered. But my naked frontside was vulnerable to the universe. I was drumming and master of my soul.

71. *I HAVE A FIFTH ALTAR (6-23-1992)*

  I dreamt I had a fifth altar. (The other four are: the Christian, the Jewish, the shamanic altar, and the altar of individuation.)

  And I myself was that fifth altar. I was the monstrance; I was the mass. I was the chapel; I was the tabernacle; I was the burning candle bringing light into the darkness.

72. *I AM A SPECKLED SHAMAN (6-26-1992)*

  I dreamt I was a shamanness, sitting on the earth wrapped in my prayer shawl. All around me were women. I was speckled. And I was leading the liturgy.

73. *THE RED EARTH CATHEDRAL (7-26-1992)*

  I dreamt that I was shown a book about an ancient place of pilgrimage, a cathedral built of rose-colored sandstone. Since time immemorial the gypsies had gone there to worship, to ask for grace and healing. I was shown their baptismal fountain, beautifully carved from red sandstone. The gypsy women liked to drink from it and wash their long black hair in it because the water came from deep inside of the earth. I saw the fountain from the side and it looked like a delicate tau, like a capital letter "T." But I knew that seen from above, it had the shape of a large rose. The water ran out of the fountain through fine spouts set into full oval shapes that resembled eggs. Suddenly I found myself stepping into the picture. Everything became real and alive for me. I could see, hear, feel, sense, and taste the reality. It was part of my life, and I was a part of it all.

  The next thing that I was shown was the close-up of a hand belonging to a statue of a woman carved from natural white sandstone and a long poem about "eating the incense." The gypsies would come to the statue on their pilgrimages. The woman held in her right hand "green ruffled herbs," that is, sage. The pilgrims would bend over the hand and eat the natural incense from it to purify their whole being—body, mind, soul and spirit—before entering the red cathedral. During the night the statue of the herb giver would come alive to pick the sage fresh for the pilgrims. Again I found myself stepping into the picture. Everything became real and true. I was a part of it, and what I saw was a part of my life.

  The third thing that was shown to me was a picture of the corner next to the entrance of the red cathedral. It showed three niches side by side in the wall. Suddenly there was a second set of three niches, and then maybe even a third one. Then I was shown an enlarged picture of the central niche. The niche was hollowed out of the sandstone, resembling a huge egg seen from the inside with a tiny hole on top. This niche was a wind catcher, the lower half of which was black. Its upper half had been made snow-white by the wind swirling in it. It would catch the wind and the wind would swirl inside it and slow down finally to stream into the red cathedral through the tiny hole for the renewal of the air. Again everything came alive for me. I stepped into the picture. I became a part of the reality which I saw. And the reality became part of my life. I stood very still as I contemplated the wind catcher and that big cathedral built entirely from rosy red sandstone. I looked again at the rose garden and the herb garden surrounding it, at the pilgrim's path, the baptismal fountain, and the statue of the herb giver.

  When I woke up I realized that the lower part of the cathedral was built as deep into the earth as its highest tower reached up into the sky.

74. THE NEW BAPTISTERIUM BY THE OCEAN (7-31-1992)

I dreamt of a new baptisterium in the sand dunes on the shore of the ocean. The old baptisterium was changing and things were coming together in a new way.

75. A DIAMOND RING FOR MY FOREHEAD (8-18-1992)

I saw two hands working on a ring. This ring was for me. But I would not wear it on a finger. Instead it would be planted into my forehead. The ring was made of the finest, purest gold and had a stone. This was a one carat diamond in the shape of a cube. The hands cut the gold to both sides of the diamond in such a way that two wings remained. Set into my forehead the flesh would grow over the wings and the diamond would stay there forever.

76. MY BANNER OVER YOU IS LOVE (8-22-1992)

As I was incubating a dream under the starry night sky on the beach of Lake Michigan, I heard a song being sung within my being:
> I'LL TAKE YOU TO MY BANQUETING TABLE,
> MY BANNER OVER YOU IS LOVE.

77. I AM GIVEN A CROWN WITH DIAMONDS (8-22-1992)

That same night I received the vision of a crown. This crown was for me. It was made of white gold. Each peak carried a one carat diamond in the shape of a perfect cube. There was a pattern engraved into the gold. It showed high waves rising out of the ocean. That is, each peak of the crown was a wave holding up a diamond.

78. A DREAM TEACHES ME HOW TO BLESS (8-31-1992)

I dreamt that I was being taught how to bless others. I learned how to bless with my whole being, to really bless people. A voice said: "Oh, the blessing hands . . ."

79. A PICTURE FOR MY ALTAR (9-1-1992)

I dreamt that I held a photograph in my hands. It showed a charcoal painting which I had created in the dream to have a document of something important that had taken place. The picture showed the moment when I had opened the two golden cubes of Sophia and inhaled the breaths of my shaman ancestors. Together with all my dream animals I knelt in a circle on the earth around the black iron box containing both golden cubes. They were open. I framed the photograph so I would be able to hold it in my hands for meditation and to put it on my altar.

80. THE OPEN CHANNEL (9-11-1992)

Like a flash of lightning I saw a vulva on the far right side. Two big hands moved it forward in my direction and tilted it. A stream of crystal clear water fell down from it into an open channel which looked like a rain gutter. The trough was long and horizontal. I stood much lower at the very end of it and was therefore able to catch that water with my hands as it flowed out of the channel.

81. A BLACK BEAR COMES INTO MY HOME TO STAY (9-16-1992)

I dreamt that I was sitting on our bed looking at the light coming into the room through the west window, when my husband and son entered. Our son carried a baby American black bear in his arms. As soon as the little bear spotted me she jumped out of my son's arms onto the bed, ran across the raspberry-colored bedspread towards me, and climbed into my lap. She was small but solid, healthy, and round. She looked at me with trusting and loving eyes. When I contemplated her in my lap I saw that I wore a long skirt made from black bearskin. It was very elegant. The black hairs sat on the leather in little tufts that looked exactly like the small clouds around the harvest moon on my vision quest. As I petted the little bear who lay comfortably in my lap, I knew that she was hungry. When I got up and put her on the bed she began to nibble my fingertips to show me that she needed food. I left her on the bed and went downstairs into the kitchen to get her some: half a slice of whole rye bread, some milk, and a small chunk of raw meat. I also took a dish filled with fresh water because I had seen her lick her little snout and felt she was thirsty. I thought: "I must make a living space for the little bear in my house, spread a wool blanket in a corner for her, and set out a dish of water, so that she can drink whenever she wants to." And I decided to make a permanent home for the bear in my house.

82. *A WAVE CARRIES THE DIAMOND LIGHTS TO THE SHORE (9-23-1992)*

I dreamt it was night and I stood on the shore of the ocean. In the middle of the sea I saw one big wave. The water was black but carried on its frothy crest a very strong bright light which shone like a clear diamond, like a chunk of the sun. On both sides of it were many more lights getting progressively smaller towards the right and left. These, too, were shining bright like chunks of the sun. That huge wave was shaped like a crown. It was carrying the diamond lights through the darkness to the shore.

83. *I DISCOVER THE LANGUAGE THAT TRANSCENDS ALL BARRIERS (9-26-1992)*

I dreamt that I was somewhere in England or Ireland but did not know how to speak the language of the native people. I met a young girl with whom I longed to communicate. We were standing near each other when I realized that I could collect all my thoughts into my heart and then reach out to her with the heart. As I did this and my heart came closer and closer to hers, I beamed my thoughts right into her heart and she heard me. A dialogue without words ensued, an unspoken communication. As I touched her heart with mine, I was filled with joy because I had discovered the language that transcends all language barriers.

84. *A PRIEST OF THE OLD RELIGION INCUBATES DREAMS TO HELP THE PEOPLE (9-27-1992)*

I dreamt that many people brought their problems and questions to a priest of the Old Religion. He would take these questions with him into the sanctuary of the gods and use them as incubation phrases. Dreams would come to him during sleep, which contained the answers to the questions of the people. After each vision quest he would come back to the people and tell them the dreams. A voice said: "They go and ask their gods and come back with the answers."

85. *MY LEFT HAND IS BLACK (10-16-1992)*

I dreamt that the Black Madonna stood behind me and held my left hand in her very large black hand. When I looked at our hands together, I saw that my hand and my whole arm were black. The skin was of a deep golden black color.

86. *THE BLACK MADONNA STANDS BEHIND ME AND SUPPORTS ME (10-31-1992)*

I dreamt I saw a finished charcoal drawing in front of me. It was titled "The Crown." The word "crown" meant that energy radiated from the heart, the forehead, the top of the head, and both hands of the woman in the painting.

Another dream came to me during the same night. I dreamt that the Black Madonna was standing behind me and supporting me. She held my hands up by the wrists so that the palms were facing towards the people.

87. *FOUR BIG HANDS HOLD A LARGE CROWN (11-7-1992)*

I saw four big hands holding a very large crown. The two hands in the back were black, the two hands in the front white. It was the shaman's crown.

88. *I MUST BE A SERVANT OF THE LIFE FORCE (11-12-1992)*

I dreamt that I was called to serve the light, that I was a servant of the life force. I was working for the life force and for the people. I dreamt this dream twice.

89. *I AM A PRIESTESS OF THE BLACK MADONNA (11-27-1992)*

I dreamt I was standing at my altar. The candles were burning. I wore priestly vestments: a long elegant flowing dress made from a dark fabric dotted with tiny stars. That dress looked as if it was a map of the living star-studded night sky.

90. *THE STONE IS A SANCTUARY OF THE BLACK MADONNA (12-27-1992)*

I dreamt that I was in a place of nature, a rocky landscape. I stood leaning against a big grey rock which was a perfect cube; my right hand rested on top of it. The stone had grown naturally. Its lower half sat in the earth. The hermits living in that area had worked on it diligently for a very long time. They had transformed the rock into a sanctuary of the Black Madonna. First they had cut an entrance into the stone and then proceeded to hollow it out, carving an altar and benches along the walls in the process. They had decorated the outside with lovely filigree patterns. And so the stone had become a holy place for the people.

91. *I AM BEING TAUGHT HOW TO INTERCEDE FOR OTHERS (1-31-1993)*

I dreamt that a woman showed me through the example of her life how to stand up for justice and intercede for people. She taught me by letting me see how she did this. This woman stood before the inner powers against injustice and for humanity. She used all of her own powers to help the people. She would put her whole heart into pleading their causes. Sitting on a chair she lost herself in pleading to such an extent that her body folded over and bent lower and lower until her voice was only a whisper and head and hands touched the ground. I watched this process with full attention. When she was folded to the ground, I knelt down before her. I gently touched her right hand with mine in such a way that I scooped her fingertips up with my own and asked: "And did it help?" She looked me straight in the eye and her face was so radiant that it seemed as if light flashed from it. She responded: "Yes, yes!" She raised herself and stood up. Her whole body was radiant. Again she said: "Yes, yes!"

And from then on, whenever I saw that someone was helpless or treated unjustly, I opened all the channels. Putting my whole heart into the pleading I turned to the source and simply asked: "Help, please, help, please, help, help!" just as my teacher had done.

92. *THE HOLY ROCK SHINES LIKE GOLD (3-9-1993)*

I dreamt I saw a huge round stone in the twilight. It shone like gold because the sun illuminated it. A voice said one should stand together with the Black Madonna and one's loved ones before the Holy Rock and move in a circle or spiral around it.

[C. G. Jung once was asked:] "What is the criterion that indicates whether an archetypal dream or a vision should make an obligatory demand on an individual, or be evaluated only as an expression of a general contemporary event which the dreamer has picked up and which does not address him as an individual human being?" [He answered:] "The desired criterion here is whether the dreamer feels numinously addressed by the dream. If not, then it doesn't concern him—and it doesn't concern me either. At most it could initiate a theoretical bandying about of words, which of course is futile."[2]

CHAPTER 18

Shaman of the Black Madonna

The great decisions in human life usually have far more to do with the instincts and other mysterious unconscious factors than with conscious will and well-meaning reasonableness. The shoe that fits one person pinches another; there is no universal recipe for living. Each of us carries his own life-form within him—an irrational form which no other can outbid.

—C. G. JUNG,
The Practice of Psychotherapy[1]

haman of the Black Madonna is a series of thirteen charcoal drawings done between April 26 and June 6, 1992.

166

165. See Overleaf

166. Tataya also dreamt that she was to contemplate her death and spend time on this important matter. She found herself in a church chanting the "Dies irae" from the Latin Mass for the Dead. When she took a look at the corpse in the open coffin before the altar, she saw it was herself.

165

165. One day in 1989 Tataya experienced a physical symptom that signaled to her the onset of menopause, commonly called ''the change of life.'' During the following night dreams spoke to her of inner death and spiritual renewal. She dreamt of a big bear with blessing hands who demanded her freedom. She knew the ancient secret of transforming an ordinary tree into a precious fruit-bearing one.

167

167. Later the same night Tataya dreamt that grave robbers had discovered the burial site of one of her male ancestors in Siberia who had been a shaman. They found his drum, abalone shell, and many other ritual objects in the ground which she claimed for herself. In the grave of her ancestress Sophia, Tataya discovered a black iron box that held two cubes fashioned of pure gold. When she opened them she involuntarily inhaled the breaths of her ancestors that had been preserved in them. As these breaths flowed into her, they made her a shaman of the old tradition.

168

168. In those dreams Tataya experienced her shaman-ancestors as living powers. They were delighted that the shamanic bloodline had not died out with them and that the gift had surfaced in Tataya. They desired for her to continue the work, that is to devote her life to the Holy, to looking after nature and to consoling and helping the suffering souls that would touch her.

169

170

171

169. Before the shaman-ancestors had passed away they had been told by the spirits that Tataya would come, claim her inheritance, and continue the ancient tradition. Their last thoughts had been of her. They had seen her in visions and blessed her.

Tataya is aware that the mysterious things which are taking place in her life now are connected to her childhood dream in the same way that the blossoms of a tree are one with the roots. In her first dream she had found safety and meaningful work in the realm of the Black Madonna and had thus been shown the essence of her entire life. She is conscious that the Great Mother carries her now as then, and that her life has no other meaning but to serve the Divine Spirit in Nature.

170. Through much inner work Tataya has matured from reluctance to obedience. She obeys her dreams now and her awareness of the Transpersonal Psyche, having learned the truth of what C. G. Jung expressed: "But vocation acts like a law of God from which there is no escape."[2]

Many dreams have told her that she can journey to any place in the inner world via a channel of pure light. Led by her drum, the heartbeat of Mother Earth, and pushed by the powerful hands of the Black Madonna Tataya, together with her dream animals, travels upwards inside the Tree of Life. As they journey, the tree grows higher and higher and pushes its tip, the Monstrance of the Black Madonna, into the brilliant White Light of God high up in the sky.

171. The Divine Light is home of the Holy Trinity and the Blessed Mother who lives there since the day she ascended with body and soul into Heaven and was crowned Heavenly Queen. Altogether there are now four persons lovingly connected in the Divine realm. The Holy Quaternity consists of God the Father, God the Son, God the Holy Ghost, and the Mother of God. As the dazzling light of the Trinity shines on the Blessed Mother, her back lies in the shadow and is black. This is the point where the Monstrance of the Black Madonna works its way into the Godhead. The Monstrance carries the Earth. And so the ego-Self axis between God and Nature has established itself; the gulf is bridged.

172

173

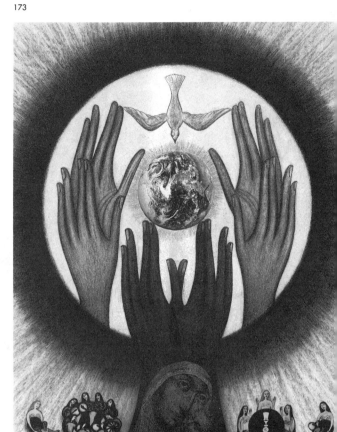

172. All the Blessed Mother has to do when the monstrance touches her is to turn around and take a look at what is there. And as she does so, her face and her whole being are in the shade and she stands black, ancient, and wise surrounded by the blinding light of the Trinity. Tataya sees clearly with her own eyes that the Blessed Mother and the Black Madonna are one and the same person. God the Mother bends down, picks up her beloved monstrance and puts it in the center of the Quaternity. She calls the attention of the Father, the Son, and the Holy Ghost to the world, encourages them to admire her exquisite beauty and grandeur, and demands that they cherish her totally. And so the Earth has ascended into Heaven, one could also call this state of wholeness "Heaven on Earth."

173. The Great Mother now has much work to do, but it is a labor of love. She enlightens the Holy Trinity about the forgotten life-giving powers residing in the land, the oceans and rivers, the mountains, the air, the fire, plants and trees, the animals, the children, the dreams, visions, and much, much more. She makes the Holy Trinity fall in love with the life force hidden in matter, the mind inside Nature. The Father, the Son, and the Holy Ghost had never paid much attention to it, as it did not seem important enough compared to Heaven. In fact they had found it bothersome at times. But now the innocence, the colors, the native intelligence, and the magnificent wealth of the Black Madonna's treasure move them so deeply that they cannot take their eyes off the world. Their acceptance fills the heavenly realm with a joy and harmony not known there in quite this way before.

174

174. The Great Mother celebrates her mass for God the Father, God the Son, and God the Holy Spirit. They are all gathered around her host which is the world. Holding the Earth in her hands God the Mother says: "This is my body." For Holy Communion each person of the Quaternity eats two hosts, that is, they eat nature twice.

The animals too have ascended into Heaven via the channel of pure light inside the Tree of Life. They appear black in contrast to so much light. But in reality they are the innocent ones, who add color, a change of pace and feeling, a new way of looking at life, and a lot of vitality to the heavenly realm. For that they are dearly loved and appreciated.

175

176

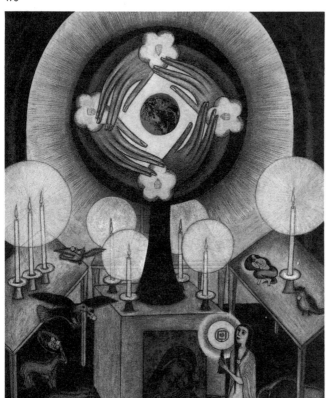

175. This picture shows Tataya in her own underground chapel. She has brought the monstrance of the Holy Quaternity back with her and put it on her altar of individuation. It is surrounded by Tataya's other three altars: the Christian altar, the Jewish altar, and the shamanic altar. All the candles are lit. Tataya's dream animals bring white roses in their mouths and are content.

176. Tataya has dreamt that four naked women balanced the Earth on their outstretched hands above their heads, and she saw them carry the planet into a church. Suddenly the Black Madonna rises out of the light which streams through the windows into the church illuminating the earth. But perhaps it is the other way around and light radiates from the Earth through the church out into the world.

177. This picture is a portrait of Tataya in her room. She sits on a pillow before an Earth altar. Next to her are her drum and lantern. She has just lit sage, cedar, and sweetgrass in her red abalone shell and smudges herself with a feather.

Tataya likes to set up altars from the dreams. These change all the time, depending on the symbols that come up and need to be given a body. This particular dream

altar honors the Monstrance of the Black Madonna and symbolizes Tataya's inner situation. The Sacred Pipe on the rainbow cloth in the center stands for the ego-Self axis, that is, it symbolizes the open channel between the realms of the Transpersonal Psyche on one side and ego-consciousness on the other. The former is expressed by the dream picture and the shining lights, the latter by a clear crystal standing on a square mirror that sits in a polished round silver plate.

Setting up altars like this is a form of inner work. Tataya learned to embody her dreams through sandplay. Two of the Jungian analysts with whom she worked taught her how to give visible shape to dreams in a sandbox. Not having one of those wonderful sandboxes at home, Tataya makes altars. Once the dreams have a body, she can contemplate them better, because now they can be seen, touched, and circumambulated. In this way she experiences her dreams not just with the mind but with all her senses. Often this helps her grasp the meaning of a dream subliminally long before she can articulate it. When as a result of this she feels joyful and energized, she knows that she is on the right track, because "the reward of a correct interpretation is an uprush of life."[3]

177

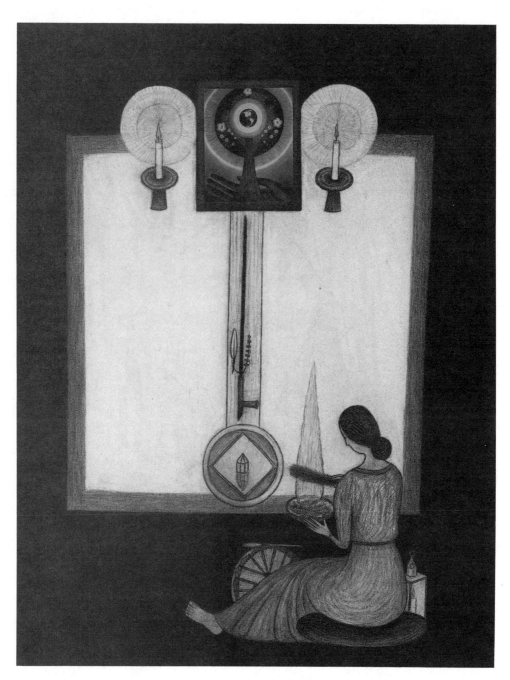

177. See previous page for text.

In order to make this idea of a Quaternity comprehensible, Jung connects it with his well known theory of the psychology of the unconscious. He roughly reasons as follows: In ancient times the devil, i. e., the unconscious, existed in direct relationship to the spirit, or the conscious. This relationship was highly beneficial; the conscious nourished with its light the shadows of the unconscious; with its positivity the negativity of the unconscious; with its rationality the instinctuality of the unconscious. The ancient religions were aware of the relationships between conscious and unconscious; and what is more, they encouraged them. . . . He concludes that it is necessary to restore as quickly as possible these relationships: and if necessary, to create precisely that Quaternity.[4]

Her Banner over Me Is Love

The dream is a little hidden door in the innermost and most secret recesses of the soul, opening into that cosmic night which was psyche long before there was any ego-consciousness, and which will remain psyche no matter how far our ego-consciousness extends. For all ego-consciousness is isolated; because it separates and discriminates, it knows only particulars, and it sees only those that can be related to the ego. Its essence is limitation, even though it reach to the farthest nebulae among the stars. All consciousness separates; but in dreams we put on the likeness of that more universal, truer, more eternal man dwelling in the darkness of primordial night. There he is still the whole, and the whole is in him, indistinguishable from nature and bare of all egohood.

It is from these all-uniting depths that the dream arises . . .

—C. G. JUNG, *Civilisation in Transition*[1]

er Banner over Me Is Love is a series of nine charcoal drawings done between October 3 and November 16, 1992.

178

179

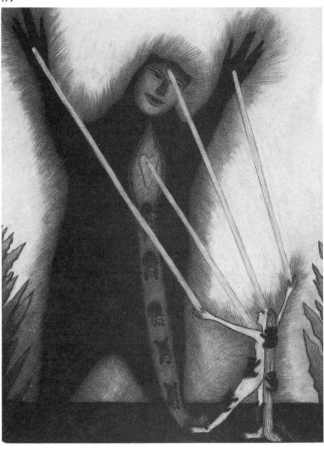

178. Tataya has dreamt of a big bear with black hands raised in blessing, who walks, thinks, and can talk in sign language. The bear wants to live with Tataya, but Tataya is afraid of a direct encounter and has kept the door between herself and the bear locked. She likes life to be simple and prefers to be left in peace. But during active imagination Tataya saw the bear behind a huge glass wall looking towards her with great expectations. And now a new dream has come in which the glass wall shatters and crashes down.

179. Tataya is a reluctant shaman. She has fought against her vocation for two decades because it seemed an irrational, impossible thing to her. She lives in a modern Western society. Who needs additional complications? Still the dreams have continued. She has dreamt that a baby black bear was cooked into stew for her and that she had to eat it. She also has had several dreams of receiving a young bear for a gift. And she dreamt several times that she was being taught how to shamanize. Now on top of all this, that big glass wall has shattered and she cannot escape the bear with the blessing hands anymore. A total energy exchange takes place. Her contact points with the bear are her heart, her forehead, and the palms of both hands. The baby black bear happily climbs all over Tataya because she is where she wants to be: Tataya has to love her now and cannot run away anymore.

180. This is a year of solitary vision quests for Tataya. On weekends she travels with her husband to a favorite spot on the shore of Lake Michigan, to an ancient Native American power place. Tataya experiences the Great Lake as an ocean because of the endless horizon and the grandeur of the waves. Out there she sleeps on a blanket in the sand and incubates dreams under the stars. Her husband keeps a nice fire going from sundown to sunrise, plays his flute, observes the night sky with his telescope, and watches over Tataya through binoculars. While the sound of the waves rocks her to sleep, Tataya feels she is in the heart of the Black Madonna. Tataya has dreamt of a new baptisterium in the sand dunes by the ocean. She has also dreamt that she catches clear water streaming towards her from a vulva through an open channel. But the most mysterious of all dreams is one in which the Black Madonna gave her a fifth shaman ring. It was made of gold and had a one carat diamond in the shape of a cube. This ring was not meant to be worn on her hands like her other four rings, but to be pressed into her forehead. In the dream she saw the hands of the Black Madonna cut the gold to both sides of the stone in such a way that two wings remained. Set into her forehead, the flesh would grow over the golden wings and the diamond stay there forever.

180

181

182

181. To incubate dreams in a place of nature is a powerful experience and different from doing it in one's bed in the city. Surrounded by the night sky, the ocean, the trees, animal cries, the wind, and the fire, one understands oneself to be a tiny fragment of the cosmos. The heart feels it. It is real. When I wake up with a dream and look up into the stars and hear the song of the waves, I know with my whole being the truth of what C. G. Jung formulated in this way: "The dream is a hidden little door in the innermost and most secret recesses of the soul, opening into that cosmic night which was psyche long before there was any ego-consciousness, and will remain psyche no matter how far our ego-consciousness extends."[2]

182. I then can give myself over to the dreams and flow with them. I can let the Black Madonna sing to me: "I'll take you to my banqueting table, my banner over you is love." I can accept that she puts a ring into my forehead and gives me a crown fashioned of white gold, engraved with a pattern of high waves rising out of the ocean with one carat diamond cubes on each peak. I can listen to her when she wants me to be the fifth altar, the monstrance, the mass, the tabernacle, the burning candle which brings light into the darkness. I don't have to run away anymore. I can accept my "blood-kinship with the rest of mankind"[3] as Jung calls it, I can just let it be.

At home, back in the city, I can then honor the dreams and contemplate them, give them a body in my pictures, and altars, circumambulate them, amplify them, compare them with the visions of other people on the planet, and finally understand them. I know then, that the dreams mean the soul, that they speak in symbols and metaphors: priestly vestments, altars, ceremonies, and jewelry are symbols for the development of personality. The dreams do not tell me to dress up or play a role. Provided I earnestly do the necessary inner work, the moment will come when I understand the messages of the dreams and can do them justice. Then my life will be what the Transpersonal Psyche wants it to be.

183. Tataya has dreamt, that she must be in this world but not of this world, and that she is related to the Holy. In a dream she saw a rose tree. It bloomed in a symphony of reds: innumerable red hues reaching from rosy pinks and variegated oranges over fiery reds and blood reds to magentas and deep violets. The Black Madonna said to her: "Love is the one indestructible power in the universe." On her vision quests she sings with the waves, the wind, and the stars to the Great Mystery:

With Thy Sweet Soul, this soul of mine
Hath mixed as Water doth with Wine.
Who can the Wine and Water part,
Or me and Thee when we combine?
Thou art become my greater self;
Small bounds no more can me confine.
Thou hast my being taken on,
And shall I not now take on Thine?
Me Thou for ever hast affirmed,
That I may ever know Thee mine.
Thy Love has pierced me through and through,
Its thrill with Bone and Nerve entwine.
I rest a Flute laid on Thy lips;
A lute, I on Thy breast recline.
Breathe deep in me that I may sigh;
Yet strike my strings, and tears shall shine.[4]

183

184. Tataya saw this picture in her dreams exactly the way it is painted here. In her active imaginations now sometimes traditional songs and prayers come up, like the prayer of Saint Francis, transformed according to her dreams:

Mother, make me an instrument of your peace.
Where there is hatred, let me sow love;
Where there is suffering, healing;
Where there is despair, hope;
Where there is darkness, light;
Where there is stagnation and rigidity, new life;
Where there is fear, inner stillness;
Where there is loneliness, the brother- and sisterhood of
the Earth.

O Loving One, let your face shine on me;
Abide with me in the visions of the night;
Hold me in the pure space of Your Heart
And in your Blessing Hands forever.

Mother, you who are the numinous mystery of my inner
world,
Grant, that I may not so much seek
To be consoled as to console,
To be understood as to understand,
To be loved as to love;
For it is You who makes me whole,
Who helps me flow in a sacred way with life
And who strengthens me to stand up for the Earth and the
living things.

185. This is Tataya on one of her vision quests by the ocean. She has a new circulatory system made of light. Her new heart drives that light in her body and soul. She now knows that what she once considered her monster and painted as a black octopus inside herself, moving her limbs with its tentacles, was the Ineffable tormenting her from within. It was the spiritual darkness within her, torturing her to become conscious, having no other place to bring forth light but this poor human being in which it dwelt. Tataya is looking out over the ocean, where one big wave has risen. It has the shape of a crown and carries on its crest strong bright lights that shine like clear diamonds. These diamond lights are so bright that they dazzle her like chunks of the sun. Soon they will reach the shore.

186. Tataya has dreamt several times that a crown is given to her for the people. Now a new dream has come in which four large hands held a huge crown towards her: the shaman's crown.

During the day, as she goes about her workaday duties, Tataya often hums a song to the Great Mystery. She uses the transformed text of an old hymn[5] to express her love for the Ineffable and sings the words to the tune of the Adagio from Beethoven's *Emperor Concerto:*[6]

There is a wideness in your mercy
Like the wideness of the sea.
There is a kindness in your justice
Which is more than liberty.
There is welcome for the wayward
And more graces for the kind.
There is mercy flowing freely.
There is healing in your mind.

There is no place where our sorrows
Are more felt than in your heart.
There is no place where our frailties
Can more freely be a part.
There is plentiful forgiveness
For the ones who humbly pray.
There is joy and there is healing.
You will show us all the way.

For the love you show is broader
Than the measure of the mind.
And your heart with love eternal
Is most wonderfully kind.
When you speak in dreams and visions,
I embrace you heart in heart.
And I cleave to your abundance,
We will never be apart.

184

185

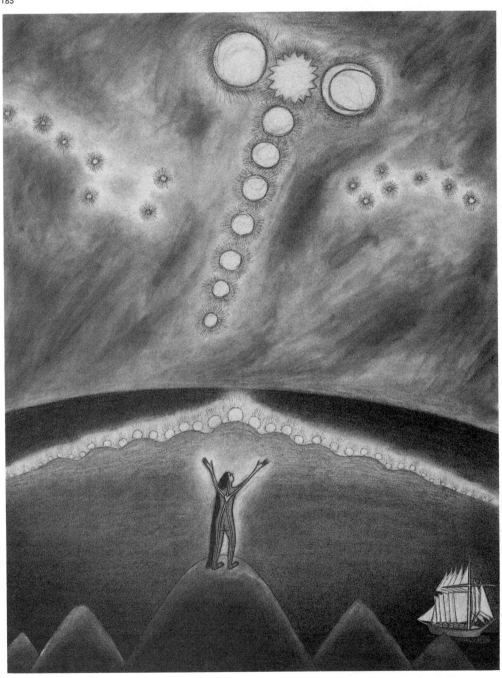

186

CHAPTER 20

I Sleep but My Heart Waketh

When you observe the unconscious you come across plenty of instances of a very peculiar kind of parallel events. For example, I have a certain thought, or a certain subject is occupying my attention and my interest. At the same time something else happens, quite independently, that portrays just that thought. . . . There is a probability, it is something more than chance that such an event occurs.

—C. G. JUNG,
C. G. Jung Speaking[1]

I *Sleep but My Heart Waketh* is a series of five charcoal drawings done between November 17 and December 11, 1992.

187. When life puts me in difficult situations and I do not know what to do, I incubate dreams, because I remember that "The unconscious mind of man sees correctly even when conscious reason is blind and impotent."[2] Every time dreams come to help me. They offer me creative solutions to my problems which I would never have thought of myself. But the deepest and most sacred dreams have come to me during vision quests on the shore of Lake Michigan.

187

188

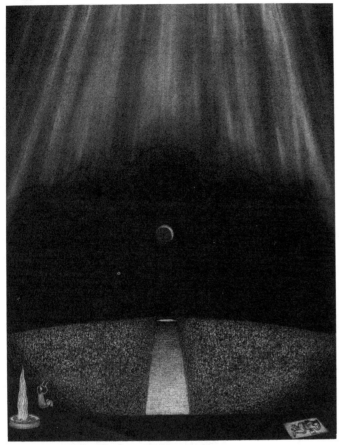

189

188. During the vision quests Tataya's husband keeps a fire going and scans the night sky with telescope or binoculars while she sleeps on a blanket in the sand, pen and pad next to her. Tataya stalks the dreams. She has trained herself not to move when she wakes up in order to see the dream images as long as possible. While her eyes remain closed and her body still, the hands write her dream down.

Amazing synchronicities have happened on the vision quests. Once, during a warm night in June of 1992, the northern lights appeared in the sky over the sea, waving back and forth like a huge white curtain or sail billowing in the wind. Tataya remembered what the Black Madonna sang to her in a dream: "I'll take you to my banqueting table, my banner over you is love." And it was a sign to her that the Black Madonna was indeed spreading Her veil over Tataya and the people for protection and healing as the dreams had promised.

189. During that same night another synchronistic event took place. Tataya and her husband had gotten out of their car not far from her place of the vision quests, on a blacktopped street that runs through hills. The land all around them sparkled with fireflies. It looked as if the earth was dotted with a thousand tiny stars exactly as the sky above. The northern lights appeared again, but this time over the horizon. They looked like five constantly changing beams of white light. The rays grew taller and taller until their tips met high in the sky. To Tataya it looked as if the Sacred Lodge of White Buffalo Woman was growing out of the Holy Land. She called out to her husband: "Look, the Tipi of Reconciliation!" At that moment a big bolide [a large, brilliant meteor] streaked through the starry sky.

190

190. Tataya loves to sit on a rock by the ocean in all kinds of weather and watch the moon rise out of the water. The Great Mystery sings to her in waves, clouds, and wind. And Tataya answers with her heart. Sometimes she then sings an old church hymn, the words of which she has paraphrased for herself:

> I heard your voice, Great Mystery, say,
>   "Come unto me and rest;
> And in your weariness lay down
>   Your head upon my breast."
> I came to your presence as I was,
>   so weary, worn and sad;
> I found in you a resting place,
> And you have made me glad.

> I heard your voice, Great Mystery, say,
>   "Behold I freely give
> The living waters, thirsty one,
>   Stoop down and drink and live."
> I came to your presence and I drank
>   Of that life-giving stream.
> My thirst was quenched, my soul revived,
>   And now I live your dream.

> I heard your voice, Great Mystery, say,
>   "I am this dark world's light.
> Look unto me, your star shall rise
>   And all your night be bright."
> I looked to your presence and I found
>   In you my moon and sun.
> And in that light of life I'll walk
>   Till pilgrim days are done.[3]

191. Tataya likes to amplify her dreams and inner experiences by linking them with those of other people on the planet. C. G. Jung used to do that all the time. For instance, when she had painted this picture from her dreams, she came across a poem by Lao Tzu, who lived about 2300 years ago. A long time ago she had copied it into her volume of *Grimms' Fairy Tales.* She had forgotten about it. But now she saw that Lao Tzu's soul knew the Great Mystery in much the same way as she:

> The men of the world are merry-making,
> As if life were an endless feast,
> The world a terrace in springtime.
> I alone am still. I wait.
> Like a new-born babe, unsmiling,
> I appear homeless, forlorn.
>
> The men of the world have riches;
> I alone go emptyhanded.
> I seem to others witless,
> Unheeding, vague—a fool.
>
> The men of the world are knowing;
> I seem unenlightened.
> They are clever, sharp, alert;
> I am reserved and silent,
> Motionless as the sea.
>
> The men of the world are useful;
> I am a tool outworn.
> But—alone and different—
> I am nourished at the Holy Breast
> By the divine one, the Mother-Spirit.

191

A dream that is not understood remains a mere occurrence; understood, it becomes a living experience.

—C. G. JUNG[4]

AUTHOR'S AFTERWORD

Black is the absence of color, there is no black in a rainbow," someone recently said to me. But I was not convinced. To me black has always been the most mysterious and expressive of all colors. When I was a child, we often burned a candle in the evening to save electricity. After a while the flame would rise high and smoke badly. The wick needed trimming. Once in a while I then would take a dinner plate and hold it over the flame to catch the soot out of the hot trembling smoke. The child saw the color black being born before her very own eyes and was delighted.

For the little girl this was a "living black" which had so many shades and was connected to a piece of life that she loved. She did not like the "dead black" of her grandmother's handknit wool stockings and the dresses of never-ending mourning, of her aunt's heavy habits and the priests' cassocks, of catafalques, prayerbooks, and laquered coffins. But she adored the iridescent feathers of grackles in the cherry tree, shadows playing on the ground, wood burning to a crisp in the hearth, the star-spangled night sky around the moon, sweet black currants picked into her little apron, freshly turned soil sprinkled with apple blossom petals, the soft coat of a black rabbit in her lap, a placid pool deep in the woods during autumn time-rippled by raindrops, mirroring golden trees and the sun above. Even today I feel beguiled when I contemplate blue damselflies hovering between reeds over black swamp water or a double rainbow shining on the background of stormclouds in the summer sky. Nothing can convince my heart that black is not a color, even though the dictionary says otherwise. I only have to look at the lovely skintones of black people in my neighborhood and at the dreams in which the hues of the Black Madonna's complexion have varied from ebony over blackberry, chocolate, honey, and wheat to moon light. She is *black* because she is colorful. She is *life,* mysterious, everchanging *eternal life.*

Little Tataya sitting before the fire in her grandmother's kitchen would have died of joy had she known that someday she would belong to this sacred Mother who would bring many siblings into her life: brothers and sisters, not only the family of man, but the whole extended family of all living beings on the planet. And that she would be a part of them, love them and call them "All My Relations":

> a relative I am . . . a relative to all that is . . . all over the earth the faces of living things are all alike. With tenderness have these come up out of the ground . . .
> I was seeing in a sacred manner the shapes of all things in the spirit, and the shape of all shapes as they must live together like one being. And I saw that the sacred hoop of my people was one of many hoops that made one circle, wide as daylight and as starlight, and in the center grew one mighty flowering tree to shelter all the children of one mother and one father . . .
> And beneath it all the animals were mingling with the people like relatives and making happy cries . . .
> And I saw that it was holy.[2]

Had the child been able to look into the future she would have seen a greater life ahead of her, would have seen her destiny unfold and herself as an old woman on vision quests in a country far away. That woman nowadays just loves to sit silently next to her husband in the light and warmth of a nice big fire on the shore of Lake Michigan listening to its crackle and the rhythm of the sea behind it. The waves sing to her of the Great Mystery and life simply lived. They rock her soul into an altered state of consciousness, an inner place, where she opens herself to the dreams and abandons herself to the Black Madonna in her heart. This is her sacrament.

My true homecoming into the family of humankind and all of life happened when through the practice of dream incubation I found out that the roots of all living beings are intertwined and that a deep contact from soul to soul is possible during the dream state. We are all subliminally connected and can intercede for each other. With some practice one can learn to turn inward and come together with others on that inner level. In this way we can solve problems. We can comfort each other when afraid, help each other when hurting. We can console, heal, and bless one another over any distance. It is a Holy Communion beyond anything I could ever have imagined.

C. G. Jung knew this kind of bond which he called "the Golden Thread." He said that this form of relationship is "the only lasting one, in which it is as though there were an invisible telegraph wire between two human beings."[3] The dreams tell me that many people can link up with each other via the Self in this manner, to help one another as spiritual relatives and to heal the suffering Earth.

All the time I carry a vision in my soul, a wild hope in my heart. I see individuals all over the planet set out upon "the great adventure of individuation, the journey to the interior."[4] They devote themselves to inner work and gather around the Black Madonna within. Standing like trees on solid ground inside themselves on that "patch of inner eternity"[5] which not even death can touch, they become guardian angels of the Earth for these troubled times. Great dangers are threatening the planet and our survival. Hard times are in the making for all of us. Each individual needs to become "a brother seeking out his brothers."[6] We need to weave golden threads of spiritual connectedness. In my vision I see brothers and sisters all over the globe linking up into a spiritual safety net for the world. Perhaps C. G. Jung foresaw this in his last dream, when he dreamt of trees the roots of which reached around the Earth and of golden threads glittering among those roots.[7]

Dreams and active imaginations have brought healing to me. I am free in my soul. I feel alive and at home in the inner world as well as in the outer. To be healed though does not necessarily mean to be cured. Simone Weil expressed it well: "even the grace of God himself cannot cure irremediably wounded nature in this world. The glorified body of Christ bore the marks of nail and spear."[8] The fact is that my life looks to me just like that old tattered cloak in a poem from the twelfth century. It is so beaten and has so many holes that all it is good for is to look through it and beyond it to the stars.

> I HAVE A CLOAK THAT IS LIKE A SIEVE TO SIFT
> WHEAT OR BARLEY. I SPREAD IT OUT LIKE A
> TENT IN THE DARK OF NIGHT, AND THE STARS
> SHINE THROUGH IT: THROUGH IT I SEE THE MOON AND THE
> PLEIADES, AND ORION,
> FLASHING HIS LIGHT. I AM TIRED OF COUNTING
> ALL ITS HOLES, WHICH ARE SHAPED LIKE THE
> TEETH OF A SAW. NO THREAD CAN HOPE TO
> MEND ITS GAPS WITH WARP AND WOOF. IF A
> FLY LANDED ON IT WITH ITS FULL WEIGHT, IT
> WOULD QUICKLY REGRET ITS FOOLISHNESS.
> O GOD, GIVE ME A ROBE OF GLORY IN
> EXCHANGE—THIS WOULD BE PROPERLY
> TAILORED![9]

I love my life and am content with it. It is the only one I will ever have. I am used to it and it is precious to me. No matter how threadbare and frayed it is, I am comfortable with it because it is mine. C. G. Jung once was told, that his psychological insights and his attitude to the unconscious resembled those of shamans. He happily answered: "Well, that's nothing to be ashamed of. It is an honor!"[10] He was well aware that shamans are wounded healers.

Knowing intimately and personally the realm of sickness, decrepitude, dying and death readies the shaman for his or her actual mission . . . the healing of person and society in relation to the greater cosmos . . . By dying in life, the shaman passes through the gates of fire to the realm of eternally awakened consciousness. Having tasted immortality, the laughter of compassion wells up from the human heart. The suffering that the shaman endures, then, gives rise to the realm of play, for the shaman is both in *and* out of the field of life. The faces of many shamans are riven with suffering and lined with laughter. The Trickster, the Wise Fool, emerges to dance the forces of nature, to sing the songs of creatures, to dream the way of the future.[11]

I imagine C. G. Jung would simply say that although we cannot become free of suffering, we do not have to suffer blindly anymore. He would also tell us, that "anything good is expensive. It takes time, it requires your patience and no end of it."[12]

> *The experience of the Self brings a feeling of standing on solid ground inside oneself, on a patch of inner eternity which even physical death cannot touch.*
>
> —MARIE-LOUISE VON FRANZ,
> *C. G. Jung: His Myth in Our Time*[13]

NOTES

FOREWORD

1. Deepak Chopra, M.D., *Quantum Healing: Exploring the Frontiers of Mind/Body Medicine* (New York: Bantam Books, 1990), p. 158.

CHAPTER 1: *Dreams Become Meaningful in Unexpected Ways*

1. See Carl G. Jung, *Man and His Symbols* (New York: Doubleday & Company Inc., 1972), p. 23.

2. C. G. Jung, *Psychological Reflections: A New Anthology of His Writings 1905–1961* (Princeton, NJ: Princeton University Press, 1973), p. 97.

3. See Barbara Hannah, *Jung, His Life and Work: A Biographical Memoir* (New York: G. P. Putnam's Sons, 1976), p. 94.

4. C. G. Jung, *Letters*, Vol. 1: 1906–1950, ed. Gerhard Adler and Aniela Jaffe (Princeton, NJ: Princeton University Press, 1973), p. 377. *Numinosum* (the numinous) is the Latin term for the awe-inspiring mystery, the Holy. A numinous experience is electrically charged with a sense of the sacred and causes a change of consciousness because of its emotional power.

5. Jung, *Psychological Reflections*, p. 200.

6. C. G. Jung, *Psychology and Alchemy, Collected Works*, Vol. 12, ed. Herbert Read, Michael Fordham, Gerhard Adler, and William McGuire (Princeton, NJ: Princeton University Press, 1963), par. 50. (*Collected Works* hereafter cited as CW.)

7. Jung, *Psychological Reflections*, pp. 85–86.

CHAPTER 2: *My Childhood Dream*

1. From a letter written by C. G. Jung to P. W. Martin, 20 August 1945 (original in English). In C. G. *Jung Letters*, Vol. 1: 1906–1950, ed. Gerhard Adler and Aniela Jaffe, Bollingen Series XCV: 1 (Princeton, NJ: Princeton University Press, 1973), p. 377.

2. *Shamanism in Siberia*, ed. V. Dioszegi and M. Hoppal (Budapest: Akademiai Kiado, 1978), p. 510.

3. Barbara G. Myerhoff, *Peyote Hunt: The Sacred Journey of the Huichol Indians.* Symbol, Myth, and Ritual Series (Ithaca, NY: Cornell University Press, 1974), pp. 78–79.

4. Alice Miller, *Banished Knowledge: Facing Childhood Injuries* (New York, NY: Doubleday, 1990), p. 167.

5. Mircea Eliade, *The Forge and the Crucible* (London: Rider & Company, 1962), p. 79.

6. Eugen Drewermann, *Kleriker: Psychogramm eines Ideals* (Olten und Freiburg im Breisgau, Germany: Walter–Verlag, 1990), pp. 47–60.

7. Johann Wolfgang Goethe, *Faust: Der Tragoedie zweiter Teil* (Stuttgart, Germany: Philipp Reclam Jun., 1972), p. 11.

8. See Morris Berman, *The Reenchantment of the World* (New York, NY: Bantam Books, 1988), pp. 229–30.

9. See Mircea Eliade, *Shamanism: Archaic Techniques of Ecstasy,* Bollingen Series LXXVI (Princeton, NJ: Princeton University Press, 1974), p. 4.

10. See Sogyal Rinpoche, *The Tibetan Book of Living and Dying* (Harper San Francisco, 1992), p. 81.

11. Joan Halifax, *Shaman: The Wounded Healer* (New York: Crossroad, 1982), p. 88.

CHAPTER 3: *Terrifying Experiences Lead to a Heightened Awareness of the Transcendental*

1. *PBS's Great Performances: Spirituals in Concert,* "Kathleen Battle and Jessye Norman sing American Spirituals at Carnegie Hall," Sound Recording by Deutsche Grammophon, 1991.

2. Carl Sagan, *Cosmos* (New York: Random House, 1980), pp. 336–37.

CHAPTER 4: *First Active Imaginations*

1. Marie-Louise von Franz, *C. G. Jung: His Myth in Our Time* (New York: Little, Brown and Co., 1975), p. 230.

2. See Lillian B. Rubin, *Worlds of Pain: Life in the Working-Class Family* (New York: Basic Books, 1976).

3. C. G. Jung, *Alchemical Studies,* CW 13, par. 20.

CHAPTER 6: *The Octopus and the Black Madonna*

1. C. G. Jung, *The Structure and Dynamics of the Psyche,* CW 8, par. 181.

CHAPTER 7: *The Suffering Black Madonna*

1. See Edward F. Edinger, *The Creation of Consciousness: Jung's Myth for Modern Man* (Toronto, Canada: Inner City Books, 1984), pp. 105–7.

CHAPTER 15: *My Personal Myth*

1. C. G. Jung, *Memories, Dreams, Reflections,* ed. Aniela Jaffe (New York: Vintage Books, Random House, 1965), p. 325.

2. C. G. Jung, *Man and His Symbols* (New York: Doubleday & Company, 1972), pp. 160–62.

3. Jung, *Memories, Dreams, Reflections,* p. 3.

4. Edward F. Edinger, *The Bible and the Psyche: Individuation Symbolism in the Old Testament* (Toronto, Canada: Inner City Books, 1986), p. 48.

5. Anne Maguire, "Jung's First Dream" in *Betwixt & Between: Patterns of Masculine and Feminine Initiation,* ed. Louise Carus Mahdi, Steven Foster and Meredith Little (Open Court, La Salle, Illinois 1987), p. 60.

6. Marie-Louise von Franz, *C. G. Jung: His Myth in Our Time* (New York: Little, Brown and Company; G. P. Putnam's Sons, 1975), p. 205–7.

7. Jung, *Man and His Symbols,* p. 165.

8. C. G. Jung, *Psychology and Religion: West and East,* CW 11, par. 252.

9. South of Eagle, Wisconsin, on Highway 67 there is an outdoor ethnic museum named "Old World Wisconsin." Of particular interest here is the room called the "Black Kitchen" which is an old-fashioned Pomeranian country kitchen covered with black soot from the open fireplace. The kitchen is one of the rooms in an authentic house built by immigrants to Wisconsin from Pomerania (now part of Poland).

10. Morton Schatzman, *Soul Murder: Persecution in the Family* (New York: Signet New American Library, 1974), pp. 133–46.

11. George Ryley Scott, *Flagellation: A History of Corporal Punishment in Its Historical, Anthropological and Sociological Aspects* (London: Tallis Press, 1968).

12. Eugen Drewermann, *Kleriker: Psychogramm eines Ideals* (Olten und Freiburg im Breisgau, Germany: Walter-Verlag, 1990).

13. See Joan Halifax, *Shaman: The Wounded Healer* (New York: Crossroad, 1982) and also Ean Begg, *The Cult of the Black Virgin* (New York: Routledge and Kegan Paul Ltd., 1986), p. 92.

14. See C. G. Jung, *Symbols of Transformation,* CW 5, par. 428.

15. See Marija Gimbutas, *The Language of the Goddess* (San Francisco: Harper and Row, 1989), pp. 319–20.

16. See C. G. Jung, *The Archetypes and the Collective Unconscious,* CW 9, par. 446, and Jung: *Memories, Dreams, Reflections,* p. 313.

17. Marija Gimbutas, *The Language of the Goddess,* p. 321.

18. Joseph Campbell, *The Power of Myth* (New York: Doubleday, 1988), pp. 91, 190.

19. C. G. Jung, *Symbols of Transformation,* CW 5, par. 374 and 484.

20. See Jung, *Symbols of Transformation,* CW 5, par. 128 and 388.

21. Edward F. Edinger, *The Christian Archetype: A Jungian Commentary on the Life of Christ* (Toronto, Canada: Inner City Books, 1987).

22. *The Complete Grimms' Fairy Tales* (New York: Pantheon Books, 1972), pp. 133, 151, 249, 530, 664.

23. See C. G. Jung, *Alchemical Studies,* CW 13, par. 256, 257 and 300.

24. Edward F. Edinger, *The Creation of Consciousness* (see chap. 7, n. 1).

25. C. G. Jung, *C. G. Jung Speaking: Interviews and Encounters,* ed. William McGuire and R. F. C. Hull (Princeton, NJ: Princeton University Press, 1977), pp. 188–89.

26. C. G. Jung, *Psychology and Religion: West and East*, CW 11, par. 148.

27. Edward F. Edinger, *Ego and Archetype: Individuation and the Religious Function of the Psyche* (Baltimore, MD: Penguin Books Inc., 1973), p. 7.

28. Edinger, *The Creation of Consciousness*, pp. 53–54.

29. See Edinger, *Ego and Archetype*, p. 105.

30. Simone Weil, *The Simone Weil Reader*, ed. George A. Panichas (New York: David McKay Company Inc., 1981), p. 487.

31. See Edinger, *The Creation of Consciousness*, pp. 105–6.

32. Jung, *Man and his Symbols*, p. 162.

33. See Jung, *Psychological Reflections*, pp. 85–86.

CHAPTER 16: *My Personal Shield*

1. Jung, *Memories, Dreams, Reflections*, p. 3.

2. Gimbutas, *The Language of the Goddess* pp. 113–19.

3. Joseph Campbell, *Transformations of Myth through Time* (New York: Harper & Row, 1990), p. 9.

4. Heinrich Imhof, *Rilkes "Gott"* (Heidelberg, Germany: Lothar Stiehm Verlag, 1983), p. 141.

5. Johann Sebastian Bach, *Motetten: Jesu meine Freude* (Wolfenbuettel, Germany: Moeseler Verlag, no date), p. 13.

CHAPTER 17: *Excerpts from My Dream Journals*

1. C. G. Jung, *Civilisation in Transition*, CW 10, par. 318.

2. *C. G. Jung Speaking*, p. 370.

CHAPTER 18: *Shaman of the Black Madonna*

1. C. G. Jung, *The Practice of Psychotherapy*, CW 16, par. 81.

2. C. G. Jung, *The Development of Personality*, CW 17, par. 300.

3. C. G. Jung, *Two Essays on Analytical Psychology*, CW 7, par. 189.

4. *C. G. Jung Speaking*, pp. 188–89.

CHAPTER 19: *Her Banner over Me Is Love*

1. C. G. Jung, *Civilisation in Transition*, CW 10, par. 304f.

2. C. G. Jung, *Civilisation in Transition*, CW 10, par. 304f.

3. Jung, *Civilisation in Transition*, CW 10, par. 306.

4. Poem by Jalalu 'd Din (1207–1273), in Evelyn Underhill, *Mysticism*, (New York: E. P. Dutton, 1961), p. 426.

5. See Hymn No. 470, from *The Hymnal 1982* according to the use of The Episcopal Church (New York: The Church Hymnal Corporation, 1982).

6. Ludwig van Beethoven, Concerto No. 5 in E-flat Major for Piano and Orchestra, Op. 73, Second Movement: Adagio un poco mosso.

CHAPTER 20: *I Sleep but My Heart Waketh*

1. *C. G. Jung Speaking*, p. 314.

2. C. G. Jung, *Psychology and Religion: West and East*, CW 11, par. 608.

3. See Hymn No. 692, from *The Hymnal 1982* according to the use of The Episcopal Church, New York 1982.

4. C. G. Jung, *The Practice of Psychotherapy*, CW 16, par. 252.

AUTHOR'S AFTERWORD

1. C. G. Jung, *Psychology and Religion*, CW 11, par. 167.

2. John G. Neihardt, *Black Elk Speaks: Being the Life Story of a Holy Man of the Oglala Sioux* (New York: Pocket Books, 1972), pp. 5, 29, 36.

3. *C. G. Jung Speaking* p. 31.

4. von Franz, *C. G. Jung: His Myth in Our Time*, p. 287.

5. von Franz, *C. G. Jung: His Myth in Our Time*, p. 74.

6. Ludwig van Beethoven, *Fidelio*, Act II, Scene 2.

7. See von Franz, *C. G. Jung: His Myth in Our Time*, p. 287.

8. *The Simone Weil Reader*, ed. George Panichas, p. 444.

9. Poem by Abraham ibn Ezra, *The Penguin Book of Hebrew Verse*, ed. T. Carmi (Philadelphia: Penguin Books, 1981), pp. 353–54.

10. von Franz, *C. G. Jung: His Myth in Our Time*, p. 13.

11. Halifax, *Shaman: The Wounded Healer* (see chap. 2, n. 11), p. 92.

12. E. A. Bennet, *C. G. Jung* (London: Barrie and Rockliff, 1961; New York: E. P. Dutton, 1962), p. 152.

13. von Franz, *C. G. Jung: His Myth in Our Time*, p. 74.

INDEX

References to key phrases and images from active imaginations and dreams have been indexed when they occur in the text and in captions throughout the book, but not when they occur in the complete listing of active imaginations and dreams in chapter 17. In most instances, if readers look up one of the index entries for a dream image, they will find given in the text the number of the dream as listed in chapter 17. (In order to keep consciously worked on material distinct from unconscious material, active imaginations and dreams have been indexed separately.)